WOOD FIRED FEAST

OVER 100 RECIPES FOR THE WOOD-BURNING OVEN

JON FINCH

WOOD FIRED FEAST

OVER 100 RECIPES FOR THE WOOD-BURNING OVEN

JON FINCH

THE GUILD OF MASTER CRAFTSMAN

PUBLICATIONS

INTRODUCTION

I've cooked in wood-fired ovens for well over a decade now, using everything from portable tabletop models right up to huge custom-built Italian masterpieces, some of which were big enough to cook a whole pig, perhaps even two. Each type of oven differed in terms of length of time it took to heat up, the amount of fuel it used per hour, and residual heat and fire placement. But, essentially, they all did the same thing, just in their own way.

Over the years I have experimented with cooking all kinds of things in wood-fired ovens and have ultimately concluded that pretty much anything you can cook on a barbecue, a smoker or in your regular kitchen oven can be cooked every bit as successfully in a wood-fired oven.

I've been running wood-fired oven classes for DeliVita for a couple of years now and each one has its own theme: diner classics, Mexican, from the ocean, tapas, etc. There's a class for almost everything apart from pizza! It was a conversation with Joe Formisano, the DeliVita founder, many months ago that gave this book the spark of life. He loved the fact that the class menus were so varied, creative and diverse, yet everything was relatively straightforward to cook; and that, through the classes, we were helping his customers and dealers to truly unlock the potential of their wood-fired ovens. He suggested we should write a book capturing everything we were doing so that it could help wood-fired oven cooks everywhere discover the true potential of their wood-fired ovens. All the dishes in this book were cooked in a DeliVita oven, but the recipes work equally well regardless of the brand or type of oven you are using.

I don't know many other bits of kit that are as versatile as a wood-fired oven. I want people to break out of the mindset that their oven is just for pizza. You'll notice that most people refer to their ovens as 'pizza ovens', but they are so much more! I love pizza as much as the next man (which is why there's a pizza section in this book), but for every 20 times I fire up my oven, perhaps only one of those is for pizza. So, get out in the garden, experiment with different styles of cookware, ingredients and cooking temperatures, and have fun with it!

Now, if you are looking for a good place to jump in with both feet, I recommend having a go at The Perfect Steak (page 126). This showcases how a wood-fired steak not only matches the quality of a steak grilled on a barbecue or indoors in a pan, but how it surpasses both. It's the best of all worlds: we're cooking in cast iron, so the heat retention is terrific, giving a beautiful all-over sear; we're getting the real flavour of woodsmoke as the flames lick the meat; plus, we're able to add butter, herbs and garlic to the dish as it cooks. It's the best steak ever.

COOKING
WITH FIRE

CHOOSING YOUR WOOD

The wood you choose will have a big impact on the flavour and aroma of your dishes, as well as your overall cooking experience. Certain woods burn hotter and faster, other types a little cooler but more consistently and for longer.

Most hardwoods and fruit woods are good to use in a wood oven. Or mix them up a bit: use a base fuel, such as oak, silver birch, beech, ash, alder or olive, and then add fruit woods, such as apple, pear, walnut or cherry, for extra flavour. My favourite wood to cook with is silver birch. It's a great all-rounder with a lovely aroma, decent heat and burns for a good while.

I like to burn kiln-dried logs, as they are easier to light and give off far less smoke. Wood with a high moisture content is no fun for anyone. If you are burning regular logs, ensure they have been 'seasoned' or stacked and stored somewhere dry for at least a year.

Avoid softwoods. They have a high sap content and will give off a bitter, acrid flavour and aroma, as well as coating the inside of your oven in a thick layer of sticky, sooty stuff.

Never use treated, painted, glued or salvaged wood. These will undoubtedly contain chemicals that will not only create nasty flavours as they burn but could also be very dangerous.

BUILDING YOUR FIRE

I've found that the best way to create a good base fire in a wood-fired oven is to use the upside-down 'Scandi' method. It goes against the commonly held views on how to build and light a fire, but it works incredibly well and requires a lot less fiddling around and hands-on babysitting to get the fire going. It's also a terrific way to light a fire pit or log-burner.

In this method, the bigger pieces of wood sit at the bottom, the medium-sized wood is next, then the thinnest kindling, and the firelighters perch right on top.

This may seem strange – we all grew up building fires the opposite way round – but it means that the fire gradually burns downwards, each layer dropping embers and igniting the next layer down with the biggest logs at the bottom eventually igniting. It avoids the need to keep adding wood as the fire builds.

Very importantly, you must stack each layer of wood at 90 degrees to the one below it and leave plenty of gaps for airflow. Think of it like building a small, wonky Jenga structure and you won't be far off.

You should always use eco-firelighters in your oven, rather than any derived from petrochemicals. The eco ones are generally made from wood shavings and vegetable wax and won't taint the flavour of the food.

Build your fire near the entrance to your oven, then just before you start cooking, push it to the back or side, depending on your set-up.

KEEPING THE FIRE GOING

There's no set rule on how often you need to add logs to the fire. Each wood-fired oven will have a different burn rate, depending on size, insulation, ambient weather, the temperature you are trying to maintain and, of course, the type of wood you are burning. I've used huge ovens that will quite happily eat a whole sack of logs every hour or two, and much smaller ones where a couple of decent logs, chopped into smaller pieces, will keep it going all afternoon.

A good rule of thumb, though, is little and often. Always add logs well before the fire has gone out. I prefer to add smaller logs (slightly thinner than your wrist) fairly often, rather than bigger logs.

A little-and-often approach irons out the fluctuations in heat as the fire dies back and rebuilds. There's always going to be a bit of up and down, but the more we can iron this out the better.

If you do leave it a little too late to add another log and you find it smouldering rather than catching quickly, then use a long length of copper pipe to blow air into the fire and it should ignite in no time.

OVEN MAINTENANCE

Wood ovens are fairly low maintenance and require very little attention to keep them in tip-top condition, but it is worth spending a little bit of time every now and then to show them some love.

Here are some of the regular jobs you can do to keep your oven happy.

BRUSH OUT
I only brush out my wood oven as and when it needs it, which is usually after four or five uses, or when I can see that the ash has built up to a level that will start interfering with fire lighting. Ensure the oven is stone cold with no hot embers before you start and use a soft-bristled brush to sweep out most of the ash.

VACUUM CLEAN
Once every few months, or if I am planning to cook pizza, I'll brush the oven out and then use a heavy-duty vacuum cleaner (mine's a Shop Vac) to really get rid of any residual dust and debris, and to make sure my pizzas come out as clean as possible.

KEEP DRY
The dome and floor of many wood ovens are made of clay, which can tolerate the odd splash of water but really ought to be kept dry. One sure-fire way to crack your oven is to soak the inside and then light a really hot fire in there! Buy a cover or fit a tight door for rainy days.

LOW FIRE AFTER WINTER
Even if your oven has been covered, during a long, winter without use the cold and damp is likely to have permeated your defences. In the same way that you season your new oven initially, I like to build a very small fire inside (just one or two bits of kindling) and keep it going for a few hours, just to make sure it is bone dry before I start ramping up the heat.

T-CUT
The entrance to my wood oven is made from metal, and the outer shell of the dome is fibreglass. Over time, soot and dirt can build up on these, which causes absolutely no harm to the oven, but doesn't look so pretty. I use a tiny amount of T-Cut (car paintwork restorer) on a damp cloth, just to clean up this sooty residue and bring the oven back to looking brand new again. This is purely cosmetic, of course, but it's a nice thing to do every once in a while.

KIT LIST

One of the things I love about wood ovens is their simplicity: it's fire and food, and has remained that way for many, many years. There's evidence that primitive forms of pit-style wood ovens were used as far back as 29,000 BC in Central Europe – and were used for cooking mammoth!

When it comes to kit, you can bet our ancient ancestors weren't using probe thermometers and suchlike while cooking their leg of mammoth roasts, so don't feel you need oodles of equipment to cook successfully in your wood oven. Appreciate the purity!

Having said that, we're not cavemen, and of course there's plenty of equipment out there to make our cookout days easier and more manageable. I've tried to narrow down the list as much as possible and put the items into two categories: the things I consider to be the real essentials – in other words, the items I use every time I fire up the oven; and a few things that you certainly don't need – but it's always good to have a little list of ideas at the ready when your birthday is on the horizon, right?

MUST-HAVES

POKER
You'll need a poker for pushing fresh wood into the oven and moving embers around. This will be by your side the whole time you cook, so choose a good one. My favourite is made by Alex Pole Ironworks and is a very simple but effective design. It's also beautifully made and a pleasure to use.

FIRELIGHTERS
Eco-lighters are best for your wood oven. They're natural (usually made from wood shavings and untreated vegetable wax) and burn well. Importantly, unlike traditional petrol-based lighter cubes, they do not leave a nasty residue in your oven, which can easily leach into the clay base and taint food.

INSTANT-READ PROBE THERMOMETER
When it comes to cooking meat, knowledge is power. An instant-read thermometer will not only tell you your chicken is safe to eat, but it will also allow you to cook steaks to the desired level of done-ness; tell you when lamb or pork shoulders are ready to be pulled and shredded; and even when breads are fully cooked in the middle. Wherever and whenever I cook, my trusty thermometer is always in my back pocket. I recommend the Thermapen brand. I've used them for years. They give an instant temperature reading and they are laboratory-grade accurate.

WIRE BRUSH
Not crucial if you are predominately cooking in cast iron, but if you are cooking food directly on the oven floor (making pizza or flatbreads, for example) then a long-handled wire brush is needed to dust away ash and embers from the cooking surface. Don't be tempted to blow the ash out of the way.

IRON COOKWARE

I've dedicated a whole section to cookware (see page 18), as you'll be using it for virtually everything you cook. A good place to start your collection is with a handle-free round dish, around 30cm (12in) in diameter (make sure it fits into the oven), with a lip of 3cm (1in) or so. There's very little you can't cook in one of those and you can build up from there.

LEATHER/HEATPROOF GLOVES

Cast-iron cookware is a delight to cook with, but marry it with an oven that could potentially be up to 350°C/662°F and you are working with some very hot metal. You'll need to invest in a pair of really good heatproof gloves, even welders' gloves will do the trick. They need to be heat resistant enough to be able to pick a screaming hot dish straight from the oven and hold it for a good 20–30 seconds before putting it down. Also, try to find a pair that allow a degree of dexterity while you wear them. It's frustrating to wear a pair so thick and cumbersome that it's impossible to grasp handles, etc.

GOOD TONGS

You'll use these all the time for turning food, moving food, lifting things in and out of your cookware, etc. I'm not a fan of the over-sized BBQ-style tongs, even when I'm cooking on a big grill. They make it difficult to grasp food deftly and lack the control and finesse you really need. For years I've used the OXO Good Grips brand. To make your life easier, buy two pairs so you have one pair for raw meat and seafood, and a second pair for moving cooked food around. It saves on washing-up and helps eliminate any contamination issues.

FREE-STANDING BUTCHERS' BLOCK/TABLE

Make life easy for yourself and get hold of something you can position next to your oven that's easy to prep food on. I use a cheap mobile free-standing butchers' block from Ikea and then a selection of thick wooden boards for resting hot cast-iron cookware on when it's come straight out of the oven.

NICE-TO-HAVES

OVEN THERMOMETER GUN

When you first start cooking with a wood oven it's only natural to feel the need to know the exact temperature the whole time, and that's what a laser gun will do for you. As you'll read in the Cooking Temperatures section (page 21), we cannot compare wood ovens to conventional kitchen ovens. There's no dial to turn it up and down, and certainly no way to set a fixed temperature. The fire will ebb and flow as you cook, and over the course of several uses you'll find yourself comfortable with gauging the heat between low, medium and hot, even if it feels a little daunting to begin with.

BLOWTORCH

I always have a blowtorch handy in case of a 'code red' fire situation. Sometimes a recently added log needs a bit of extra help to catch light, or the fire is smouldering and smoky and needs a flash of heat. A long piece of copper pipe can be used to blow on logs that need to catch light at the back of the oven.

CLOCHE

You will only really use a cloche if you are cooking burgers. It's certainly possible to make amazing burgers in a wood oven without one, but the 'cloching' technique – adding a little squirt of water to the hot pan and covering it so that everything steams – results in pillow-soft burger rolls and incredibly melty and gooey cheese.

COOKWARE

The trick to unlocking the true potential of your wood oven is to invest in a range of good iron cookware. Aside from flatbreads, pizzas and the like (which will be placed directly on the oven floor), almost everything you cook in your wood oven will be cooked in some sort of dish or skillet, or on a tray, so that the juices will be retained in the pan. Not only does this add flavour, but it also stops any fatty juices from ruining the floor of the oven.

Iron cookware is the best option, as it is relatively inexpensive, cooks food beautifully, retains heat well, withstands high temperatures and, once seasoned properly (see below), is easy to clean and relatively low maintenance.

SELECTING YOUR COOKWARE

I have a fairly small range of iron cookware, but the pans have been chosen with careful consideration and I can pretty much cook everything with them. It's very important, of course, to make sure that whatever cookware you choose, it fits through the oven door!

My collection is as follows:

1x 33 x 28 x 3cm (13 x 11 x 1¼in) spun-iron baking tray
2x 30cm (12in) diameter, 3cm (1¼ in) deep round spun-iron baking dish
1x 30cm (12in), 3cm (1¼in) deep cast-iron plancha plate, with small side handles
2x 22cm (8½in) diameter, 5cm (2in) deep round cast-iron skillet, with handle
1x 15cm (6in), 2cm (¾in) deep cast-iron baking dish, with small side handles

If I were to choose just one item to start my collection it would be the round spun-iron dish. Being handle-free and round, it allows me to rotate the dish in the oven, ensuring the food cooks evenly. The size is just right for most recipes.

CAST IRON OR SPUN IRON?

When someone mentions cooking with iron, most people assume they are referring to cast iron – the heavy-gauge, bombproof, all-in-one style of cookware you see everywhere. But, cast iron is not the only option: spun iron is now more readily available and does offer several benefits over cast iron.

WEIGHT
Spun iron can be made thinner than cast iron, meaning it can be much lighter. When you're moving searing, bubbling pans in and out of a wood oven, saving a little weight can often make things easier for the cook. Being slightly lighter, spun iron can be made into larger sizes without becoming unmanageable.

TEMPERATURE

Both types of ironware are designed to withstand the incredibly high temperatures that a wood oven reaches, but, being a little thinner, spun iron is quicker to heat up and cool down. However, it does not offer quite the same level of even heat distribution and retention as cast iron. For example, if I wanted to cook a thick steak, I'd opt for a cast-iron (or perhaps a thicker spun-iron) pan, as I'd want the cooking surface temperature to stay as hot as possible even after placing a big slab of cold meat onto it.

STRENGTH

Cast iron is brittle. If you've ever dropped a cast-iron pan or lid onto a hard surface, you'll know it can crack or shatter. Spun iron tends to be stronger and is more likely to dent or ding slightly, rather than break.

AESTHETICS

In my opinion, spun iron looks better. Maybe it is because most of the spun-iron cookware I have seen comes from smaller artisan manufacturers, such as Netherton in Shropshire, where master craftsmen create something individual and beautiful, as opposed to mass-produced cast-iron products.

SUMMARY

Both types of cookware have their place in your wood oven arsenal. I have a selection of both and opt for one or the other, depending on what I'm cooking. For ease, I've referred to pans as cast iron in the recipes, but you might be spun iron instead, depending on what you're cooking and what you have available.

SEASONING YOUR COOKWARE

It's important to season your cookware. Doing so creates a natural, easy-release cooking surface and helps prevent your pans from rusting. Seasoning involves oiling the surface of the pan and 'baking' it in a conventional oven. The more you use your iron pan, the thicker the layer of oil becomes and, as the patina develops over time, the better your pan becomes.

If you have a new pan that you want to give a head start, or perhaps an old pan that has gone a little rusty and needs re-seasoning, the manual seasoning process is very easy. Take a cold, dry pan, wipe it with a thin layer of flaxseed or vegetable oil and place it in a cold oven. Heat the oven to around 225°C/437°C, bake the pan for an hour, then switch off the oven. Leave the pan to cool slowly in the oven. Once cool, remove and store in a dry, well-ventilated place.

COOKING TEMPERATURES

The first, very important point to make here is that wood-fired oven cooking is essentially cooking with a small bonfire! We don't have dials to turn or a thermostat to help regulate the temperature. It's just us and a log fire, the temperature of which will fluctuate throughout the cooking time.

The best way to think about temperatures when cooking in a wood-fired oven is in broad bands. You will very quickly learn to roughly gauge (even without a thermometer) what level of heat your oven is running at and how much wood needs to be added to roughly maintain the heat and ensure it's sitting within a particular band's parameters.

Here's a guide to the oven temperature symbols used in this book. It gives the level of heat they indicate, a very rough comparable range in Celsius and Fahrenheit, the style of cooking each temperature range is used for and some example dishes.

	Description	Temperature Range	Style of Cooking	Example Dishes
	Very Hot	330°C+/626°F+	Fast baking	Pizzas, flatbreads, naans
	Hot	250–330°C/482–626°F	Grilling	Steak, fish, chops, prawns
	Medium Hot	200–250°C/300–482°F	Roasting	Joints of meat, chicken, root vegetables
	Medium	150–200°C/300–400°F	Slow baking	Brownies, S'mores
	Low	90–150°C/194–300°F	Slow cooking/ braising	Lamb shoulder, beef stew

Low, medium, medium hot, hot and very hot are all you need to know; 10 or 20 degrees either way is not going to make much difference. As long as you are not cremating your food, the recipes in this book are fairly forgiving and the dishes will happily cook within quite a broad range of temperatures – sometimes a dish will cook slower, sometimes quicker. We're cooking until the food is done, not to timescales or using exact cooking temperatures, as we just cannot control those. I think this is one of the reasons Aga fans love their Agas – it's less to worry about.

Clearly, the nearer to the fire your food sits, the hotter it will be, so if you find it's cooking too quickly, move it further from the flame, or even resting halfway out of the door. You can also place a bit of foil over the food to help shield it from the direct heat, or, if you're using a round dish, rotate the food as it cooks.

Once you get your head around this way of cooking, it is quite liberating. Don't stress over precise oven temperatures by using a laser gun. Instead, open another beer and accept the fact that the food will be done when it's done – just don't burn it or let your fire go out.

Most wood-fired ovens come with a door, which allows you to restrict and regulate the airflow, and insulate the oven. Closing the door retains the heat, which is perfect for baking breads and slow overnight cooks. Rake the embers out over the base of your oven for a more even heat distribution when cooking this way.

COOKING MEAT & FISH

An instant-read probe thermometer makes life much easier when it comes to checking that meat is cooked through, or to your liking. Use the following guide to help you get it right every time.

Type of meat/fish	Degree of done-ness	Internal temperature
Beef/Lamb	Rare	48°C/118°F
	Recommended	52°C/126°F
	Medium	60°C/140°F
	Well done	68°C+/46°F
Pork Chops	Rare	54°C/129°F
	Medium	60°C/140°F
	Recommended	63°C/145°F
	Well done	68°C+/154°F
Chicken/Turkey		75°C/167°F
Slow-cooked meats		92°C/198°F
(briskets, lamb shoulder, pork shoulder)		
Fish		63°C/145°F

It's important to remember that meat will continue cooking for a little while after it is removed from the oven. Regardless of the type of meat, I always recommend that it should be well rested. The bigger the piece of meat, the longer it needs to rest: a piece of fish will need a few minutes; a steak, five to ten minutes; and a chicken or roasting joint, a good 15 minutes.

BRUNCH

SHAKSHUKA

What finer way to ease yourself gently into a Sunday than with a big simmering dish of classic North African and Middle Eastern shakshuka? Not only does it taste delicious and is equally nutritious, but its hangover-easing properties are legendary, especially when paired with steaming hot, strong black coffee.

Shakshuka literally means 'a mixture' and you should bear that in mind when preparing the dish: you don't have to be too fixed when it comes to the component parts, and feel free to ad lib depending on what's in your fridge. The onions, tomatoes and, of course, the eggs must be present, but I've had it served with all kinds of things, such as crumbled feta or finely chopped spring onions. You can also make additions to the sauce – chopped peppers work very well, and so does butternut squash.

My version uses one of my favourite ingredients – rose harissa – to give that punchy, chilli background heat and vivid colour, but feel free to use any spices commonly used in Middle Eastern or North African cooking, such as cumin, paprika or chilli powder.

150–200°C
300–400°F

Serves 2

INGREDIENTS

rapeseed oil, for cooking
1 onion, diced
1 red pepper, deseeded
 and diced (optional)
1 garlic clove, crushed
1 x 400g/14oz can chopped
 tomatoes
1 tbsp rose harissa paste
4 medium eggs

To serve:
small bunch of coriander or
 flat-leaf parsley, chopped
Toasted Bread (page 52)

METHOD

Add a glug of oil to a cast-iron dish. Add the onions, pepper (if using) and garlic, then slide into the oven.

Cook for 4–5 minutes, or until softened, stirring regularly so that nothing burns.

Add the chopped tomatoes and harissa. Stir well and return to the oven.

Simmer gently for 5–6 minutes, or until the sauce starts to thicken ever so slightly.

Bring the dish out and allow to cool for a few seconds.

Make four wells with the back of a spoon and carefully break an egg into each one (it's easier to break the egg into a small dish first, then tip into the shakshuka).

Slide back into the oven for 5 minutes or so, until the egg white is set and the yolk is still runny.

If it starts to burn on top, cover loosely with foil until the eggs are to your liking.

Top with coriander or parsley and serve with toast.

TEXAS HASH

This is everything we love about Texan food: it's unapologetically big, bold and packed with flavour. It's not the most sophisticated dish, but it's a cracking way to start the day. Or end the day for that matter.

METHOD

Add the onion, pepper and garlic to a deep cast-iron dish, along with a splash of oil. Slide into the oven and sauté until softened.

Add the beef and stir well. Continue to cook until the beef is no longer pink.

Add the rest of the ingredients and give it a good stir.

Return to the oven and continue cooking, stirring often, for about 15 minutes, or until all the water has been absorbed.

Garnish with a sprinkle of parsley.

**150–200°C
300–400°F**

Serves 4

INGREDIENTS

oil, for cooking
1 red onion, finely diced
1 red pepper, diced
1 garlic clove, crushed
500g/1lb 2oz lean beef mince
1 x 400g/14oz can chopped
  tomatoes
200g/7oz/1 cup basmati rice
1 tbsp tomato puree
1 tbsp Worcestershire sauce
1 tsp chilli flakes
500ml/18fl oz/2 cups chicken
  stock
pinch of Maldon sea salt

To serve:
small bunch of flat-leaf parsley,
  chopped

MIGAS

Start your day Tex-Mex scramble style with this hearty, nutritious dish. Originally a hunter's breakfast, migas is said to have originated in southern Spain, and is a quick and easy dish to rustle up on a bleary Sunday morning to put a spring back in your step and set you up for the day ahead.

An authentic migas would use stale bread or leftover corn tortillas fried until crispy, but quite honestly, I usually just use leftover tortilla chips.

Top off your migas with a bit of whatever you fancy, or whatever you find lurking at the back of your fridge. Anything that goes well with tacos or burritos will work well, such as sliced avocado, finely sliced chilli, spring onions, sour cream, diced red onion or chopped coriander.

**150–200°C
300–400°F**

Serves 4

INGREDIENTS

oil, for cooking
8 large eggs
splash of double cream
½ tsp cumin
pinch of Maldon sea salt
couple of grinds of black pepper
1 white onion, finely diced
2 red chilli peppers, finely sliced
2 garlic cloves, crushed
2 large handfuls of tortilla chips,
 smashed up a little
200ml/7fl oz/scant 1 cup salsa
 (either leftover Scorched Salsa
 [page 203] or shop-bought)
handful of Cheddar, grated

To serve:
toppings of your choosing (see
 right for a few ideas)

METHOD

Whisk together the eggs, cream, cumin, salt and pepper.

Lightly oil a cast-iron skillet. Add the onion, chilli (reserving a little to garnish) and garlic. Sauté for a few minutes until soft.

Add the egg mixture. Return to the oven for a few minutes, mixing around regularly until they form soft curdles.

Mix in the tortilla chips, salsa and cheese and continue cooking just long enough to heat through.

Remove from the oven and garnish with the reserved chilli and the rest of your lovely toppings. In my case, it's diced red onion, avocado and coriander.

PEA, MINT & FETA FRITTATA

**150–200°C
300–400°F**

Serves 2–3

INGREDIENTS

rapeseed oil, for cooking
6 large eggs
200g/7oz feta, drained and
  crumbled into chunks
130g/4½oz/1 cup of frozen peas,
  defrosted
small bunch of mint, stalks
  discarded and leaves roughly
  chopped
Maldon sea salt
freshly ground black pepper

This reminds me of long family lunches in Italy: a table full of food and always a frittata of some description sitting in the middle, using up what's been hanging around in the fridge. Mint aside, you've probably got the rest of the ingredients sitting at home right now, but if not, I encourage you to freestyle a bit and use what's in the fridge. We love courgettes instead of the peas, for example. It's equally great hot or cold.

METHOD

In a large bowl, whisk together the eggs.

Add the feta, peas and mint, along with a pinch of salt and a few grinds of black pepper.

Mix everything together until evenly distributed.

Preheat a skillet in the oven, then add a glug of rapeseed oil.

Tip the egg mixture into the skillet and move it around with a fork for about 30 seconds, to incorporate the curds that will instantly form when the mixture hits the hot pan.

Slide the pan into the oven until cooked through (a knife or skewer inserted into the centre should come out clean).

CLASSIC ONION FRITTATA

This is equally delicious, simple and quick to make. If you can find them, it is worth hunting out Italian Tropea red onions. They are by far the sweetest and very best onions in the world – just a wonderful ingredient.

My wife loves this dish so much that one year, I contacted an Italian vegetable importer and sourced a whole crate of Tropea onions for a surprise for her birthday (there were other gifts, of course). As it turns out, after having the error of my ways pointed out to me by the entire family, onions are not a particularly suitable birthday gift for your wife. Anyway, on with the recipe...

150–200°C
300–400°F

Serves 2–3

INGREDIENTS

100g butter

4 large red onions (Tropea, if you can find them, or have been given a crate of them for your birthday), sliced

pinch of sugar

6 large eggs

Maldon sea salt

freshly ground black pepper

METHOD

Preheat a cast-iron skillet or dish.

Add the butter, onions, sugar and a pinch of salt.

Cook gently for around 20 minutes until the onions have cooked down and become very soft, and all the liquid has cooked out of them.

Beat the eggs in a bowl and add a pinch of sea salt and a grind or two of black pepper.

Add the hot onions straight from the pan into the egg mixture and mix well until all the ingredients are evenly distributed.

Add the mixture back to the skillet and stir around with a fork for 30 seconds or so, to incorporate the curds that will instantly form when the mixture hits the hot pan.

Slide back into the oven until cooked through (a knife or skewer inserted into the centre should come out clean).

MUSHROOMS ON TOAST

This is a dish I love to cook when I know I have a day of wood-oven fun ahead. Get the oven going early and make yourself this quick and tasty snack to set you off in the right direction.

The type of mushroom used is down to personal preference. I quite like the bigger, meatier mushrooms, such as ceps or portobellini, but if you want to show off, pick up some mixed wild mushrooms – the differing colours, shapes, textures and sizes look great in the final dish.

Butter is what's working the magic here, so don't try and skimp on it.

 **250–330°C
482–626°F**

Serves 1

INGREDIENTS

50g/1¾oz/scant ¼ cup butter
250g/9oz/scant 3 cups
  mushrooms, roughly chopped
5–6 sprigs fresh thyme
1 garlic clove, crushed (or 1 tsp
  garlic puree)
1 portion of Toasted Bread
  (page 52)

To serve:
small bunch of flat-leaf parsley,
  chopped

METHOD

Preheat a cast-iron skillet.

Add half the butter to the skillet and slide into the oven.

Once melted, add the mushrooms and cook for 5–6 minutes until softened and most of the liquid has cooked out.

Add the rest of the butter, the thyme and garlic and cook for a further 2–3 minutes.

Add the mushrooms to the toast and garnish with parsley.

BAKED EGGS
WITH SPINACH, ASPARAGUS & PROSCIUTTO

Eggs and spinach are a classic breakfast combo. They are usually served on a lightly toasted English muffin, and generally billed as Eggs Florentine on menus.

Well, this recipe takes all the best bits of Eggs Florentine and makes it even better in two ways: firstly, we're adding prosciutto and asparagus; secondly, we're cooking it in a wood oven.

This is one of my wife's favourite dishes and I'd really love you to give it a go.

METHOD

Add the asparagus to a cast-iron skillet with a few splashes of water and slide into the oven for a few minutes to soften.

Remove the asparagus from the pan and set aside, then add a couple of handfuls of spinach and pop back into the oven just long enough for it to wilt. Set aside.

Slice the bread loaf into four 4cm/1½in-thick slices (yes, really thick). Make the sliced bread into toast, as per the recipe on page 52.

When the toast is ready, it's time to assemble. Place the slices of toast on a cast-iron baking tray. Use the back of a ladle or large spoon to make a big crater in the top of each slice of toast. Add a small amount of cheese to the bottom of the divot, then some spinach and a few pieces of asparagus.

Carefully break an egg into each spinach nest.

Top each slice of toast with two slices of prosciutto, draping them around the sides of the nest.

Sprinkle with a little more cheese and slide into the oven until the egg whites are set and the yolks remain runny. Season with salt and pepper.

**150–200°C
300–400°F**

Serves 4

INGREDIENTS

1 bunch of asparagus, trimmed
  and cut into 2.5cm/1in pieces
150g baby spinach leaves
1 soft white loaf (classic
  farmhouse or bloomer style)
4 medium eggs
couple of handfuls of grated
  Gruyère
8 rashers of prosciutto
Maldon sea salt
freshly ground black pepper

NIBBLES & STARTERS

MEXICAN CORN

Boiling sweetcorn makes it soggy and bloated but that's the way we all cook it for some reason. This classic Mexican street food is cooked and charred entirely in the oven, resulting in crunchy, sweet, tender kernels with a buttery, creamy, spicy hit.

If you are serving a crowd, it's great to lay out all the different toppings in small bowls for everyone to make their own. Experiment with different toppings and add a little of what you fancy. My kids could happily eat this every single day of the week.

METHOD

In a small bowl, mix together the mayonnaise, sour cream and garlic.

Dip each cob in water, place on a cast-iron tray and slide into the oven.

Turn regularly until the corn is cooked through and starting to brown a little (around 6–8 minutes).

Remove from the oven and brush liberally with the mayonnaise mixture.

Sprinkle each cob with feta, a squeeze of lime and a little smoked paprika. Garnish with coriander and chilli.

150–200°C
300–400°F

Serves 4

INGREDIENTS

4 cobs of corn, husks removed
75ml/2½fl oz/⅓ cup mayonnaise
75ml/2½fl oz/⅓ cup sour cream
2 garlic cloves, crushed (or 2 tsp
 garlic puree)

To serve:
200g/7oz/1 cup feta, drained and
 crumbled
2 limes, halved
smoked paprika
coriander leaves, chopped
1 green chilli, finely sliced

VERY GOOD FLATBREADS

Of course, wood-fired ovens are amazing at cooking flatbreads, pizzas and the like, but, often, flatbreads can be dry and a bit tough. This recipe incorporates a few extra ingredients over and above the basic flour-and-water recipes, which results in a much softer bread with a good chew – and it's still super simple to make and cook.

The perfect vehicle for wrapping food like kebabs or curry, these are also great to serve with dips or baked cheeses.

**250–330°C
482–626°F**

Makes 8

INGREDIENTS

300g/10½oz/2½ cups plain flour
50g/1¾oz/¼ cup butter,
 softened
185ml/6½fl oz/¾ cup milk
pinch of salt

METHOD

Mix the ingredients together until a dough forms. Knead for about 5 minutes. It will get less sticky as you knead.

Cover the bowl with a damp tea towel and rest for half an hour.

Take the dough out of the bowl and cut into 8 equal-sized pieces.

Roll each into a ball and then flatten to around 20cm (8in), using either your hands or a well-floured rolling pin.

Preheat a skillet in the oven (or place straight on the oven floor) and cook the flatbreads one by one until puffed up, starting to brown and cooked through.

Place the flatbreads in a foil pouch wrapped in a tea towel to keep them warm once cooked.

PADRÓN PEPPERS

Oh, I love these. Possibly one of the quickest and easiest little snacks you can make, but just delicious. And the fun part? Around one in every eight or nine peppers will be a hot one. Not scary hot, but hot enough to get your attention. The Russian roulette of Spanish tapas.

Plenty of Maldon sea salt at the end is a must.

METHOD

Lightly toss the peppers in the oil until just coated.

Heat a cast-iron skillet in the oven.

Add the peppers and cook until starting to wrinkle and char (just a few minutes), turning often.

Remove from the heat and immediately season with a generous pinch of salt. That's it!

**250–330°C
482–626°F**

Serves 2

INGREDIENTS

approx. 150g/5½oz Padrón
 peppers
splash of olive oil
Maldon sea salt

HALLOUMI
WITH HONEY & SESAME SEEDS

Something magical happens to halloumi when it meets a flame. The outside gets a beautiful, delicious char, while the inside softens slightly and remains lovely and succulent.

My friend Sara served this dish to me recently and I loved it. The saltiness of the halloumi mixed with the sweet honey and the savoury, nutty pop of toasted sesame seeds works a treat.

This is a terrific little appetizer that takes just a few minutes in your wood oven.

150–200°C
300–400°F

Serves 4

INGREDIENTS

oil, for cooking
2 tbsp sesame seeds
1 block of good-quality
  halloumi (approx. 250g/9oz),
  sliced into 1cm/½in-thick pieces

To serve:
honey, for drizzling

METHOD

Preheat a cast-iron skillet. Add the sesame seeds and toast until they release their aroma. Set the seeds aside.

Drizzle a little oil into the hot pan. Gently lay the halloumi slices into the pan and return to the oven for 2–3 minutes. Flip the slices over and return to the oven.

Once the halloumi has developed a nice sear on each side, remove from the oven, drizzle with honey and sprinkle with the toasted seeds.

JALAPEÑO BACON POPPERS

**150–200°C
300–400°F**

Makes 20

INGREDIENTS

10 jalapeño peppers
250g/9oz/1 cup cream cheese
10 rashers of smoked streaky
 bacon

Once you pop, you will not stop. These are crazily moreish. Always make more than you think you'll need.

METHOD

Slice each jalapeño pepper in half lengthways. Using a teaspoon, scrape out the seeds and discard.

Fill each jalapeño half with cream cheese.

Slice the streaky bacon rashers in half widthways. Wrap a piece of bacon around the centre of each filled jalapeño half.

Place the peppers on a cast-iron tray and roast in the oven for 5–10 minutes, or until the bacon is crispy.

NASU DENGAKU

A classic Japanese side dish made with aubergines glazed in miso. The translation literally means 'aubergine grilled over a fire', which is exactly how it's done in Japan.

This is definitely my go-to quick and easy dish when I have a veggie or vegan friend over for food. While it can be served as a main dish, it also makes a terrific side for other wood-fired mains.

250–330°C
482–626°F

Serves 2

INGREDIENTS

1 aubergine
1 tbsp sesame oil
sesame seeds
nigella seeds

For the glaze:
2 tbsp miso paste
1 tbsp mirin
1 tbsp honey

METHOD

Slice the aubergine lengthways into 1cm (½in) thick slices, discarding the two outermost pieces. Very lightly score the flesh on one side of each slice, ensuring you don't cut all the way through.

Drizzle the aubergine with oil then place on a baking tray. Cook until the flesh is tender (but not mushy) and starting to brown. You will need to flip the slices over once or twice.

Mix together the glaze ingredients in a small bowl.

Brush the glaze over the scored side of each aubergine slice and sprinkle with sesame and nigella seeds.

Slide back into the oven for a few more minutes.

TOASTED BREAD

250–330°C
482–626°F

Serves 4–5

INGREDIENTS

1 very good sourdough loaf
olive oil
Maldon sea salt
1 garlic clove, peeled (optional)

Now, you are probably wondering why on earth you should spend your valuable and hard-earned relaxation time reading a recipe on how to make toast! Let me explain. This is not about taking a boring, bland, shop-bought white sliced loaf and sticking it in the kitchen toaster. Yes, a toaster makes adequate toast but we are fire cooks and we know that cooking pretty much anything in a wood oven is a) more fun and b) tastier.

The starting point is to find a really good proper rustic sourdough loaf. Artisan bakers have sprung up everywhere recently so hopefully you'll have a local source. We're going to use simple seasoning and all the flavour of the wood fire to make it something incredible in its own right. The fire and smoke will not only import flavour, but also give a beautiful charred exterior with a soft, fluffy centre.

I'll make a batch of toasted bread to go alongside pretty much anything I'm cooking in the wood oven. It's a great starter in its own right, but it's also really good for accompanying main meals and scooping up puddles of sauce or dressing.

METHOD

Preheat a cast-iron tray or skillet.

Slice your loaf into 15mm (³/₄in) thick slices.

Brush each piece on either side with a little olive oil.

Place the bread onto the tray, slide in the oven and cook until browned and almost starting to char on each side.

Once cooked drizzle with a little more olive oil and a generous sprinkle of Maldon sea salt.

A delicious extra step: try lightly rubbing a peeled garlic clove over the toasted bread, just gently, making sure the bread is still piping hot. You can then use this on its own as garlic bread or as the base for all kinds of bruschetta toppings, such as Grilled Peppers (page 68).

COURGETTES
WITH GREEN SAUCE

If you grow your own vegetables, as I do, there might be times during the year when you're wondering what on earth to do with all the courgettes you've grown. Well, here's a dish I can safely say you'll be happy to eat several times a week without ever getting bored of it. It's so fresh and zingy and takes just a few minutes to make.

It's got a bit of a Mexican vibe going on with the lime juice and coriander dressing, so once the sauce has been blitzed, do feel free to add a bit of finely chopped chilli to the mix too.

METHOD

Slice the courgettes lengthways into four long batons, then slice each in half widthways so you have 8 short sticks from each courgette. Toss with a little olive oil.

Make the green sauce by blitzing the garlic, coriander and lime juice in a food processor (or smashing them with a pestle and mortar) to a loose paste.

Place the courgettes in a cast-iron dish or baking tray and roast until charred on the outside and tender in the middle.

Place on a serving platter or in a bowl and drizzle with the green sauce.

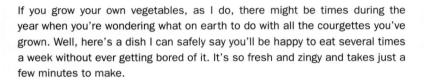

200–250°C
300–482°F

Serves 2–3

INGREDIENTS

2–3 courgettes
olive oil

For the sauce:
3 garlic cloves, peeled
large bunch of coriander
juice of 3 limes

GRILLED TOMATOES
WITH BURRATA & BASIL OIL

Right now, as I type, I'm in deepest Puglia. The Salento region in the south of Italy is where we've had a family home for a decade or more and where I first started cooking in a wood oven, albeit a really massive one that takes most of the day just to heat up and then another two days to cool down again.

Puglia is a food lover's dream and, along with the amazing fresh seafood, wine and olive oil, it's also known the world over for its burrata – a soft, creamy ball of deliciousness. If you've never tried it, externally it looks like a decent-sized mozzarella ball, but as soon as you cut into it or rip it open, a trickle of rich cream floods out and the remaining cheese is soft, unctuous and luscious.

This recipe relies on being able to source very good ingredients. There's nowhere to hide and a weak link in the chain is going to show. Find your local Italian deli or online supplier, buy the good stuff and appreciate how much a few great ingredients can make a dish sing without the need for complexity.

250–330°C
482–626°F

Serves 2

INGREDIENTS

5–6 good-sized round tomatoes
 (or a punnet of cherry tomatoes),
 on the vine
olive oil
1 burrata ball (approx. 150g/5½oz)
Maldon sea salt
freshly ground black pepper

For the basil oil:
large bunch of fresh basil,
 leaves picked
125ml/4fl oz/½ cup very good
 extra virgin olive oil

METHOD

First up, we're going to make the basil oil. Blitz the basil leaves and oil together in a food processor. Set aside in the fridge.

Quarter the tomatoes (or leave whole if using cherry tomatoes), drizzle with oil and sprinkle with a little salt and pepper.

Place the tomatoes in a cold dish or skillet, skin-side down, and slide into the oven for 5–8 minutes until slightly charred and softened.

Remove from the oven and carefully arrange the tomatoes on a serving platter.

Rip open the burrata, drizzling the creamy insides over the tomatoes. Tear the outer skin into bite-sized pieces and scatter on top.

Drizzle the dish with a few generous spoonfuls of basil oil. Finish with a sprinkle of sea salt.

STUFFED PORTOBELLO MUSHROOMS

An amazing wood-fired option for veggie friends and a nice side dish to go with meat. Feel free to experiment with a few other flavours by swapping out the basil for other herbs or spices. Sun-dried tomatoes are a nice addition, or some finely chopped crispy bacon for the non-veggies amongst you. You could also try replacing the basil and cream cheese with spinach and goat's cheese.

METHOD

Carefully slice the stalks off the mushrooms and discard. Drizzle with a little oil and place in a cast-iron skillet. Slide into the oven for 5–10 minutes until softened.

While the mushrooms cook, mix together the filling ingredients in a bowl.

Bring the mushrooms out of the oven, fill with the cheesy mixture and top with breadcrumbs.

Slide back into the oven until golden and crispy.

**200–250°C
300–482°F**

Serves 2

INGREDIENTS

2 large portobello mushrooms
olive oil
handful of breadcrumbs

For the filling:
50g/1¾oz/½ cup Parmesan
100g/3½oz/scant ½ cup
 cream cheese
small handful of basil, chopped
salt and freshly ground
 black pepper

GRILLED ROMAINE CAESAR SALAD

250–330°C
482–626°F

Serves 2

INGREDIENTS

2 romaine lettuce hearts,
 quartered lengthways
rapeseed oil
1 portion of Garlic Croutons
 (page 194)
fresh Parmesan shavings

For the dressing:
1 garlic clove, crushed
¼ tsp Dijon mustard
3 tsp Worcestershire sauce
juice of ½ lemon
1 very fresh large egg yolk
25g/1oz/¼ cup Parmesan, finely
 grated
75ml/2½fl oz/⅓ cup rapeseed oil
 or very good olive oil

The ubiquitous American salad, this dish is on restaurant menus all over the world. But did Julius Caesar really enjoy a salad that much? Of course not! As with so many of these classic dishes, it's named after the inventor, Italian immigrant Mr Caesar Cardini, who created the dish during prohibition, when he found himself in Tijuana. Yep, Caesar salad was actually born in Mexico!

Cardini's original dish was far more basic than those found today. I quite like that idea: a handful of good-quality ingredients that have the space to shine without all the fripperies, fancies and suchlike.

You'll notice a distinct lack of anchovy in this recipe. Anchovies are divisive – some people love them and some hate them. We always think of Caesar salad as being anchovy riddled (and that's not generally a bad thing, in my view) but the original was not. So, all those friends you have that never order a Caesar because of the anchovies can rejoice.

The only deviation from the original in this version is we're going to grill the lettuce for a few minutes in the oven to give it a slight char, which will add colour and texture. It looks great on the plate and it's fun to tell people you are grilling a salad for them.

As a side note, the Cardini family clearly were entrepreneurial sorts and took to bottling their famous dressing for retail. It's widely available in the UK and I can vouch for the fact it's a great pre-made dressing. So, if you want to save yourself a little bit of time, grab yourself a bottle of Cardini's!

METHOD

First, make the dressing by whisking together all the ingredients in a bowl until beautifully combined, thick and glossy.

Preheat a cast-iron tray. Drizzle each romaine quarter with oil then place in the hot tray, cut-side down, and slide into the oven for a few minutes.

Turn the lettuce hearts over. We want the two cut sides to be a little charred and starting to wilt ever so slightly.

Remove the lettuce from the oven and allow to cool for a few minutes.

Build your dish by laying the romaine quarters on a platter, scatter with the croutons and Parmesan shavings, then drizzle over the dressing. Cardini would be proud of what you've just made today.

CHORIZO & PADRÓN PEPPER SKEWERS

This is a quick and easy dish to knock up – and just so tasty! There's something magical about the paprika-loaded oil from the chorizo mixing with the charred Padrón peppers. A match made in heaven.

Be mindful of the type of chorizo you buy. The coarser ones will be trickier to thread onto the skewers. I like chorizo Riojano from the Rioja region of Spain. It's a little milder than some chorizos but absolutely loaded with paprika and, thanks to the finer texture, is easy to feed onto skewers.

As with all skewer cooking, I wholeheartedly recommend choosing flat metal skewers. They won't catch fire in the oven and the flat profile helps to stop the food spinning around when you turn them over.

 250–330°C 482–626°F

Makes 3–4

INGREDIENTS

1 whole Spanish chorizo ring
  (approx. 200g/7oz and 2.5cm/1in
  in diameter)
approx. 150g/5½oz Padrón
  peppers

You'll also need:
metal skewers

METHOD

Slice the ends off the chorizo and discard. Slice the remainder into wheels approx. 5mm (¼in) thick.

Feed alternate chorizo wheels and peppers onto the skewers. You may need to add two chorizo wheels per pepper, depending on how many peppers you have.

Place the skewers onto a cast-iron baking tray and slide into the oven.

Once the tops of the peppers have started to char and the chorizo has started to release its oil, carefully flip the skewers over and return to the oven. They'll need about 2–3 minutes on each side.

Allow the metal skewers to cool slightly and then place on a serving platter.

GARLIC & CHILLI KING PRAWNS

250–330°C
482–626°F

Serves 4

INGREDIENTS

2 tbsp rapeseed oil
500g/1lb 2oz raw king prawns,
 peeled
2–3 garlic cloves, finely chopped
1–2 red chillies, finely chopped

To serve:
juice of ½ lemon
small bunch of flat-leaf parsley,
 finely chopped

Pretty much every country with a coastline claims this dish as their own; it's as delicious as it is ubiquitous. These are great served as tapas, added into tacos or used to top a pizza.

METHOD

Preheat a cast-iron skillet.

Add the rapeseed oil and prawns to the hot pan.

Cook for a minute or two, then add the garlic and chilli.

Cook for another minute or so, moving the prawns around until they are cooked through.

Add everything to a serving dish and finish with a drizzle of lemon juice and a sprinkle of chopped parsley.

WOOD-FIRED SANGRIA

Ahh, the taste of sunny Spain, made all the better for having enjoyed the kiss of woodsmoke and the caramelization of the oranges. I've gone off-piste with the ingredients a little here, swapping the traditional brandy for passionfruit liqueur – it's a game changer.

This makes a great aperitif, but would also be an amazing accompaniment to the Spanish-influenced starters in this book, particularly the Chorizo & Padrón Pepper Skewers (page 62).

 **200–250°C 300–482°F**

Serves 4, with enough for top-ups

INGREDIENTS

2 oranges, quartered
small bowl of brown sugar
750ml/25fl oz/3 cups light, dry
 red wine
500ml/18fl oz/2 cups lemonade
50ml/2fl oz/scant ¼ cup Passoã
 (or other passionfruit liqueur)
1 ripe peach, sliced
handful of strawberries, sliced
ice

METHOD

Lightly dip the orange quarters into the sugar.

Place the oranges skin-side down in a skillet and slide into the oven until they start to char.

Allow to cool for a few minutes, then squeeze the juice through a strainer into a jug.

Add the wine, lemonade and Passoã to the jug.

Add the peach and strawberry slices.

Serve in long tumblers or large wine glasses, over ice.

GRILLED PEPPERS

This is a dish that's on rotation almost weekly in our house, and I'll always cook a batch whenever I fire up the oven. They taste even better a few days later, eaten cold. They are also an incredibly versatile ingredient to have in the fridge and are great as a toast topping, as a side to other meals, or even as an addition to stews or pasta dishes. Simplicity is the key here.

METHOD

Preheat a cast-iron baking tray.

Remove and discard the core from each pepper, then cut into quarters.

Place in a bowl, add a generous glug of rapeseed oil and mix well.

Add the peppers to the hot tray and slide into the oven.

Cook, moving the peppers around occasionally to get a nice even char.

Once the peppers have started to soften and blacken a little, remove from the oven.

Place in a serving dish, pour over a glug of extra virgin olive oil and sprinkle with sea salt.

**200–250°C
300–482°F**

Serves 4

INGREDIENTS

3–4 peppers
rapeseed oil

To serve:
extra virgin olive oil
Maldon sea salt

STREET FOOD

BEEF TACOS

This is real-deal taco-truck cuisine. It's simple but packs a whack of flavour. Don't waste expensive cuts of beef here; flank, skirt, flat iron and rump are all perfect.

The trick is to give the beef a good long soak in the marinade for an hour or two before cooking.

METHOD

In a bowl, mix together the marinade ingredients. Add the steak. Cover the bowl, or transfer to a ziplock bag, and refrigerate for 2 hours.

Get your toppings prepared and placed in little serving bowls while the meat marinates.

Fold the piece of foil in half lengthways, and then in half again. Seal three sides to create a foil envelope.

Warm your tortillas, either by placing them in a preheated skillet or straight onto the oven floor.

Once each one is warmed through, place inside the foil pouch to keep warm. (You can wrap the pouch in a tea towel for extra insulation!)

Remove the beef from the fridge and drain off the excess marinade.

Preheat a cast-iron skillet.

Tip the beef into the skillet and cook for a few minutes. (You want the beef to have a good sear and cooked to medium or rarer.)

Build your tacos with a few pieces of beef, some red onion and tomato. Add a few avocado slices, then garnish with chilli and coriander. Serve with lime wedges on the side.

**250–330°C
482–626°F**

Serves 4

INGREDIENTS

800g/1lb 12oz beef steak, cut into
  1cm/½in-thick slices

For the marinade:
2 tbsp soy sauce
juice of 1 lime
1 tbsp rapeseed oil plus a little
  extra for cooking later
3 garlic cloves, crushed
2 tsp chilli powder
1 tsp ground cumin
1 tsp dried oregano

To serve:
8 x 15cm/6in corn tortillas
½ red onion, diced
1 tomato, diced
1 avocado, thinly sliced
1 red chilli, finely sliced
handful of coriander, roughly
  chopped
lime wedges

You'll also need:
75cm/29½in-long piece of tin foil

MAC & CHEESE

This recipe is cheating a little bit as both main component parts, the macaroni and the cheese sauce, are made in the kitchen. However, the dish benefits immeasurably for having been finished off with a lick of flame and a kiss of woodsmoke from the oven. Plus, it's delicious and it makes a terrific accompaniment to so many other dishes so I thought it a shame to omit it from the book.

This recipe calls for a couple of slices of American burger cheese. While it won't add a great deal in terms of flavour, it gives the sauce a lovely colour but mainly, the natural emulsifiers found in burger cheese help stop the sauce from splitting when it cooks resulting in an outrageously gloopy and oozy end result. It's almost witchcraft, quite frankly.

It looks like a lot of cheese, but don't you worry, it will all get incorporated.

250–330°C
482–626°F

Serves 4–6

INGREDIENTS

500g/1lb 2oz/scant 4 cups elbow
  macaroni
olive oil
40g/1½oz/scant ¼ cup butter
40g/1½oz/⅓ cup plain flour
500ml/18fl oz/ full-fat milk
2 slices of American cheese
100g/3½oz/scant 1 cup mature
  Cheddar, grated
100g/3½oz/scant 1 cup Gruyère,
  grated
50g/1¾oz/⅔ cup Parmesan,
  grated
100g/3½oz/scant 1 cup
  breadcrumbs

METHOD

Cook the pasta for three-quarters of the time advised on the packet.

Rinse with cold water to cool down, drain and mix with a good glug of olive oil. Set aside.

Add the butter to a pan and set over a medium heat until it melts.

Add the flour and whisk to combine.

Leave the pan over the heat and continue mixing until it starts to colour. You're aiming for the colour and consistency of cookie dough.

Take the pan off the heat, add one-third of the milk and mix well to incorporate.

Add another third of the milk, mix well again, then return to the heat for a few minutes, whisking continuously.

Add the final third of milk and continue to cook until it just begins to simmer.

Add all the cheese, mix well and continue to cook until large bubbles appear.

Mix the pasta into the cheese sauce, then transfer to a cast-iron baking dish.

Sprinkle the top with breadcrumbs, then slide into the wood-fired oven for 5–10 minutes, or until piping hot and the top is a beautiful golden-brown colour.

SMASH BURGERS

There isn't much that can beat a really well-made classic cheeseburger in a proper diner. They are tricky to recreate at home, but with a few tips and tricks you can be making proper diner-style burgers yourself.

Unlike most burgers that are cooked as a pre-formed patty, the name 'smash burger' derives from the way that we first form the minced beef into a ball and then place it on a hot cast-iron surface and smash (well, press really) it down to flatten it out. This gives a lovely thin patty with an unrivalled sear.

First up, the meat. Start with great meat. You should be using minced beef with a meat to fat ratio of 80:20. Fat gives flavour and keeps the burger nice and juicy. If you go too lean, you'll have dry burgers – and nobody wants that.

**200–250°C
300–482°F**

Serves 4

INGREDIENTS

oil, for cooking
560g/1lb 4oz minced beef
½ small white onion, very finely
  sliced
Maldon sea salt and freshly
  ground black pepper
8 slices of American cheese

To serve:
4 brioche rolls, sliced in half
Burger Sauce (page 204)
chopped lettuce
gherkins, sliced

METHOD

Using your kitchen scales, lined with a piece of greaseproof paper, divide your meat into 140g/5oz portions (don't season the meat yet). Roll each portion gently into a ball, being careful not to compact the meat too much.

Preheat a cast-iron pan or a flat plate. Add a little oil to the pan and wipe it over the surface, using a piece of kitchen paper held with tongs.

Add 4 small piles of onion slices to the hot pan.

Put the burger balls onto the onions and press down as thinly as you can with the back of a spatula or the bottom of a pan. Each patty should be no thicker than 1cm/½in, and slightly thinner is even better.

Season with salt and pepper.

Cook for 2–3 minutes, then flip so that the onion side is facing upwards.

Cook for a further minute.

While the burgers are cooking, prepare your rolls by adding burger sauce, lettuce and gherkins to the bottom half of each one.

Add a couple of cheese slices to each patty. Add a splash of water around (not on) each burger and cover with a cloche (see page 17), pan lid or metal bowl to steam.

After 1 minute, remove the cloche and add the top half of the roll. Add another splash of water and cover with a cloche a second time.

After 15 seconds, scoop each pile off the grill with a spatula and onto the bottom half of a roll.

WINGS FOUR WAYS

150–200°C
300–400°F

Makes 24

INGREDIENTS

24 chicken wings, cut in half at
  the 'elbow' to give two straight
  bones
rapeseed oil
salt and pepper
sauce of your choosing (see
  opposite page)

Who doesn't love wings? I have a friend that judges an entire establishment just by their wings, regardless of the quality and deliciousness of the other dishes on the menu. Wings are a serious business and impossible to eat without covering yourself, your clothes and your dining companions in sauce, regardless of how many napkins you employ.

It is generally acknowledged that the original Buffalo wing was invented back in 1964 by Teressa Bellissimo, proprietor of the Anchor Bar in Buffalo, New York. There are two versions of the story behind why she invented them: one is that she received a shipment of wings rather than other chicken parts by accident and had no choice but to cook them. The other, more plausible reason in my view, is her hungry son, Dominic, and friends returned from a night on the tiles in need of a late-night snack. All that remained in the kitchen was a pile of chicken wings that were destined for the overnight stock-pot. She fried them up, slathered them with a spicy sauce, then served them with a side of blue cheese sauce and celery because that's all she had. They've been on the menu there ever since.

As well as the classic Buffalo wing recipe, I have included a few other versions that we serve on our diner menu, all equally loved by our customers. The method for making the wings in the wood oven stays the same, whichever sauce you choose – cook the wings first, then slather in sauce and serve.

METHOD

Lightly coat the wings with oil and season with salt and pepper (or your favourite barbecue rub).

Slide them into the oven, turning often, until they are cooked through, the skin has crisped up and the internal temperature at the thickest point reaches 75°C/167°F.

Put the wings in a mixing bowl, pour in your chosen sauce and mix well.

Serve with lots of napkins.

AUTHENTIC BUFFALO HOT WINGS

INGREDIENTS

300ml/10fl oz/1¼ cups Frank's Red
  Hot sauce
250g/9oz unsalted butter
3 tbsp white vinegar
½ tsp Worcestershire sauce
½ tsp cayenne pepper
¼ tsp garlic powder
¼ tsp teaspoon paprika
pinch of salt

METHOD

Place all the ingredients in a cast-iron pan, slide into the oven and heat until melted.

Remove from the oven and whisk together until combined. Allow to cool.

You may need to give it a little whisk again before covering your wings.

SRIRACHA HONEY WINGS

INGREDIENTS

250ml/9fl oz/1 cup sriracha
250ml/9fl oz/1 cup clear honey
1½ tbsp sherry vinegar
juice of ½ lime
10g/¼oz fine salt
5g/¹/₈oz black pepper

METHOD

Place all the ingredients in a bowl and mix until well combined.

BBQ WINGS

INGREDIENTS

1 medium onion, very finely diced
3 garlic cloves, crushed
180g/6oz/scant 1 cup soft brown
  sugar
500ml/18fl oz/2 cups ketchup
100ml/3fl oz/scant ½ cup
  American mustard
5 tbsp cider vinegar
5 tbsp Worcestershire sauce
5 tbsp clear honey

METHOD

Add the onion and garlic to a skillet and gently fry until soft.

Add the rest of the ingredients to the pan. Simmer for 15 minutes to thicken, adding a little water if the sauce becomes too thick.

KOREAN GOCHUJANG WINGS

INGREDIENTS

5 tbsp soy sauce
4 tbsp gochujang (Korean chilli
  paste)
1 tbsp rice vinegar
3 tbsp clear honey

To serve:
sesame seeds
spring onions, finely sliced

METHOD

Mix all the ingredients together in a bowl.

Once your wings are sauced and in a serving dish, garnish with the sesame seeds and spring onions.

PHILLY CHEESESTEAK

Some would call the Philly Cheesesteak a cultural icon and I'd agree. Born over 70 years ago at Pat's Steaks in South Philadelphia, it's a staple menu item in US diners. The authentic cheesesteak calls for ribeye steaks, surely one of the tastiest, juiciest cuts around, but also a little punchy on price. In our diner, we use the flat iron cut, or you could just as easily use bavette or even a sirloin for a good compromise option.

Whichever cut you choose, the golden rules are to shave the meat as thinly as you can, and make sure you don't overcook it.

Bread choice is also important. A traditional cheesesteak is served on a 'hoagie', a long, soft white roll. And, when it comes to the cheese, you'll need to make sure you choose a cheese that melts easily, such as provolone or mild Cheddar.

250–330°C
482–626°F

Serves 2

INGREDIENTS

oil, for cooking
1 ribeye steak, approx. 350–400g/
  12–14oz
2 soft white hot dog rolls
½ red pepper
½ green pepper
½ white onion
large handful of cheese, grated

METHOD

Slice the hot dog roll lengthways, about two-thirds of the way through, so it is still joined together. Open out like a book and lightly toast in the oven, then set aside.

Preheat a cast-iron tray or dish, lightly coat your steak in oil, then add to the dish and cook to rare (see page 126).

Set the steak aside to rest while you prepare the onion and peppers: slice the onion into half-moons, then slice the red and green pepper halves into strips.

Now, slice your steak as thinly as possible.

Splash some oil into a baking dish or tray and preheat. Add the peppers and onions and sear until starting to brown. Now add the sliced steak, mix together and cook for a few more minutes.

Now add the cheese and cloche (see page 17) until it goes all gooey, melty and wonderful.

Remove from the oven and carefully slide the bubbling mixture into your toasted hot dog rolls.

CAJUN SHRIMP SUB

250–330°C
482–626°F

Serves 2

INGREDIENTS

150g/5½oz large raw prawns,
  peeled
drizzle of oil
knob of butter
2 tbsp chipotle in adobo
150g/5½oz/scant ¾ cup
  mayonnaise
2 soft white sub or hot dog rolls
handful of shredded lettuce

For the rub:
smoked paprika
garlic powder
ground black pepper
ground white pepper
onion powder
dried oregano
cayenne pepper
dried thyme
Maldon sea salt

To serve:
smoked paprika

Cajun cuisine, known the world over for its hearty, comforting, rich and spicy flavours, arose in Louisiana in America's Deep South. Using ingredients readily available from the nearby Gulf of Mexico and the waters of the Bayou, Cajun grew to include crab, alligator, catfish, crayfish and shrimp.

One of my favourite dishes is a shrimp Po-boy, with the shrimp usually deep-fried in a heavily seasoned batter and loaded into a long, soft white roll. Well, deep-frying is one thing we don't want to attempt in our wood-fired ovens, but we can certainly hit those amazing flavour notes in a slightly different way. While the chipotle mayonnaise might seem a little bit out of place, it works a treat and emphasizes the smokiness and heat of the dish.

The rub will keep in an airtight container for several months, so it's worth making a decent-sized batch. You'll need one to two tablespoons for this recipe, but it's great added into stews, as a rub for grilled or roasted meat, or even just sprinkled onto roast vegetables.

METHOD

To make the Cajun rub, mix together equal quantities of the herbs and spices.

Add the prawns to a bowl with a little oil and 1–2 heaped tablespoons of the rub, depending on how punchy you like it. Mix well and leave to marinate for up to an hour.

Mix the chipotle and mayonnaise together and set aside.

Preheat a cast-iron baking dish, then add the prawns.

Once nicely pink and cooked through (this should take about 2–3 minutes), add the knob of butter and mix well.

Slice the rolls open like a book, load with shredded lettuce and pile in the prawns.

Finish with a good drizzle of chipotle mayonnaise and a sprinkle of smoked paprika.

TUNA MELT

A golden-crusted delight, this sandwich is stuffed with tasty tuna, has a little crunch thanks to the celery and pepper, and is covered with plenty of oozy and gooey Swiss cheese.

METHOD

In a small bowl, mix together the tuna, red pepper, celery, mayonnaise and mustard.

Spread one side of each slice of bread with a generous layer of mayonnaise.

Place one of the slices of bread, mayonnaise side down, on a piece of greaseproof paper.

Spread with the tuna mixture and top with the cheese.

Add the second slice of bread, mayonnaise side up.

Preheat a skillet in the oven, then carefully slide the cheese sandwich off the greaseproof paper and into the skillet.

Slide into the oven and cook for 2–3 minutes.

Flip the sandwich over and cook for a few more minutes.

Once the outside is golden brown and crispy, and the cheese has melted, it's done!

 **250–330°C
482–626°F**

Serves 1

INGREDIENTS

1 x 145g/5oz can of tuna

½ red pepper, deseeded and
 finely chopped

1 celery stalk, very finely chopped

5 tbsp mayonnaise, plus extra for
 spreading

1 tsp Dijon mustard

2 thick slices of sourdough bread

2–3 slices of Swiss cheese

You'll also need:
greaseproof paper, for building
 and transporting the sandwich

DeliVita

DIRTY HOME FRIES

Very similar in technique to the Parmentier Potatoes (page 186), home fries are often seen in American diners as an alternative to French fries. The idea is the same: fried potatoes with a crispy outside and fluffy inside. What's not to like, right? The benefit here is home fries are much easier to cook in a wood oven than French fries!

Mix up the toppings as you see fit. I always go for the 'more is more' approach with dirty fries.

**150–200°C
300–400°F**

Serves 4

INGREDIENTS

olive oil, for cooking
500g/1lb 2oz floury potatoes
 (such as Russet), peeled, cut into
 2cm/¾in cubes, parboiled and
 cooled

For the topping:
Cheddar, grated
crispy streaky bacon, roughly
 chopped
gherkins, sliced
Burger Sauce (page 204)
red chilli, sliced
spring onions, finely sliced
Frank's Red Hot (or other hot
 chilli sauce)
American mustard
mayonnaise

METHOD

Add a good glug of oil to a cast-iron dish or skillet and preheat in the oven.

Add the potatoes and cook until tender and nicely browned all over, moving them around in the dish regularly.

Add a handful of cheese to the potatoes and cook until the cheese melts.

Remove the dish from the oven, then add the bacon and gherkins.

Drizzle with burger sauce.

Add the chilli and spring onions.

Finish with a few splashes of hot sauce and a drizzle of mustard and mayonnaise.

GRILLED CHEESE SANDWICH

150–200°C
300–400°F

Serves 1

INGREDIENTS

knob of butter
½ leek, trimmed and sliced into
 5mm/¼in rounds
2 slices of good sourdough bread,
 approx. 1cm/½in thick
mayonnaise
American mustard
3 slices each of Monterey Jack,
 Cheddar, Jarlsberg and American
 cheese
4 slices of mortadella or good-
 quality ham, thinly sliced
2 cocktail gherkins

You'll also need:
greaseproof paper, for building
 and transporting the sandwich
cocktail sticks

A warning: this is not a grilled cheese sandwich for the faint-hearted or those looking for a healthy snack. This is a monstrous pile of oozy, gooey, cheesy, tangy, crunchy deliciousness.

If there's one thing I would love for you to take away from this recipe, it is to use mayonnaise instead of oil or butter on your grilled cheese sandwiches. It cooks out wonderfully and results in a lovely, rich, fried-bread outer layer to your sandwich. Remember: mayonnaise not butter – it's the golden rule you'll wish you'd known years ago.

You will need some greaseproof paper, but you won't be cooking the sandwich on the paper – it just makes it easier when it comes to building the sandwich and transferring it to the tray to cook.

METHOD

Add the butter and leeks to a cast-iron skillet and slide into the oven. Sauté gently for a few minutes until softened. Set aside.

Preheat a cast-iron plate or tray.

Spread a generous layer of mayonnaise onto one side of both slices of bread.

Place one piece of bread, mayonnaise-side down, onto a piece of greaseproof paper.

Spread thinly with mustard, then layer the rest of the ingredients in the following order: Monterey Jack, sautéed leeks, Cheddar, mortadella, Jarlsberg and American cheese.

Carefully place the remaining slice of bread on top, mayonnaise-side up. (You can secure the sandwich with a couple of cocktail sticks if you wish.)

Transfer the sandwich to the preheated tray, carefully sliding it off the paper and directly onto the hot tray.

Cook for 4–5 minutes, then carefully flip over using two spatulas.

Cook for another couple of minutes until the bread is golden and toasted and the cheese is unctuously gooey.

Slice the sandwich in half, transfer to a serving plate and secure the gherkins on top with a cocktail stick.

FANCY BURGERS

200–250°C
300–482°F

Serves 1

INGREDIENTS

oil, for cooking
140g/5oz minced beef
Maldon sea salt and freshly
 ground black pepper

To serve:
1 burger bun, sliced in half

Look on any diner menu (my own included) and it's likely that the list of options for burgers will be virtually endless. People top them with all kinds of crazy things.

I like to keep things a little simpler with my burgers (as I do with pizza) and use a handful of good-quality ingredients that all contribute to an overall great flavour.

Here are some of my preferred burger options to get you started. Each one follows the same method.

METHOD

Gently roll the minced beef into a ball, being careful not to compact the meat too much.

Preheat a cast-iron pan or flat plate. Add a little oil and, using a piece of kitchen paper held with tongs, wipe it over the surface of the pan.

Put the burger ball into the pan and press down as thinly as you can with the back of a spatula or the bottom of a pan. The patty should be no thicker than 1cm/½in (slightly thinner is even better).

Season with salt and pepper.

Cook for 2–3 minutes, then flip and cook for a further minute.

While the patty is cooking, slice and toast the burger bun.

Lay the bun base on a serving plate and add your base layers in the order listed.

Add the top layers in the order listed. Add a splash of water around (not on) the burger and cover with a cloche (see page 17), pan lid or metal bowl to steam.

After 1 minute, remove the cloche and add the bun lid. Add another splash of water and cover with a cloche a second time.

After 15 seconds, scoop each pile off the grill with a spatula and onto the base layers.

CLASSIC CHEESEBURGER

Base layers:
bun base
Burger Sauce (page 204)
sliced gherkins
shredded lettuce
sliced beefsteak tomato
thinly sliced white onion rings

Top layers:
patty
2 slices of American cheese
bun lid

ALL-AMERICAN DOUBLE BACON

Base layers:
bun base
baconnaise
sliced gherkins
thinly sliced red onion rings

Top layers:
patty
2 cooked smoked bacon rashers
slice of American cheese
slice of Swiss cheese
bun lid

MEXICANO

Base layers:
bun base
chipotle mayonnaise
sliced gherkins
Pico de Gallo (page 200)

Top layers:
patty
pickled jalapeño peppers
2 slices of Mexican cheese
bun lid

CALIFORNIA

Base layers:
bun base
guacamole
sprouting seeds/shoots
sliced beefsteak tomato

Top layers:
patty
2 cooked smoked bacon rashers
2 slices of Monterey Jack cheese
bun lid

LOADED DOGS

This is a great one to cook for a crowd. You can load up lots of different toppings and sauces and let everyone make their own loaded dogs. It's also very easy to cook a large number of hot dogs in your oven at once, so a great option for mass catering, too.

I like to hunt out big, fat, high-quality Polish or Balkan smoked pork sausages. They tend to be made from a much higher quality pork and they taste authentically smoked. They're far better than the skinny little ones you find in supermarkets. As with most frankfurter, hot dog-style sausages, they come pre-cooked (hot smoked), so it really is just a matter of reheating.

I like the skin on the hot dog to have a nice 'snap' to it as you eat it. This is made even better given a few minutes in a medium-hot oven, but don't go too hot or your sausages will burst.

The cooking method for all the hot dogs is the same.

200–250°C
300–482°F

Serves 1

INGREDIENTS

oil, for cooking
1 good-quality frankfurter or
  smoked Polish sausage

To serve:
1 hot dog roll
fillings and toppings of your
  choice (see below)

METHOD

Preheat a cast-iron skillet.

Add a little drizzle of oil to the pan, then add the sausage.

Cook for a few minutes.

Flip over and cook for a few more minutes, until the outside has developed a good sear and the inside has reached 70°C/158°F.

Slice the hot dog roll lengthways. Lay the cooked sausage into the roll and then go crazy with your toppings.

Some of my favourite hot dog builds are:

THE CLASSIC

Filling/topping ingredients:
finely shredded iceburg lettuce
American mustard
tomato ketchup

Build notes:
Place a layer of finely shredded iceberg lettuce into the roll.
Add the sausage.
Finish with a generous drizzle of mustard and ketchup.

GRILLED ONIONS

Filling/topping ingredients:
sliced pickles
American mustard
slow-roasted onion slices

Build notes:
Place a row of pickle slices into the bottom of the roll, followed by a squirt of American mustard.
Add the sausage.
Top with a big pile of slow-roasted onion slices.

SCORCHED DOG

Topping ingredients:
Scorched Salsa (page 203)

Build notes:
Lay the sausage into the roll.
Top with a pile of salsa.

VERY HOT DOG

There are some people that just love the kick of chilli. These are the guys that always order the hottest curry at a restaurant and slather crazy-hot sauce over everything they eat.

Back in my festival days we used to run chilli pepper-eating contests on the main stage, where everyone lined up and got issued a mild jalapeño chilli pepper that they had to eat whole. Then, they got a hotter chilli – maybe a habanero or suchlike – then a hotter one, then an even hotter one, and so on. One by one, the contestants couldn't take the pain and dropped out, gulping down milk by the jug load. The last person to drop out won ultimate bragging rights.

Well, this is the hot dog for those lunatics…

200–250°C
300–482°F

Serves 1

INGREDIENTS

oil, for cooking
1 good-quality frankfurter or
  smoked Polish sausage
200ml/7fl oz/scant 1 cup
  mayonnaise
1 tbsp chipotle in adobo (or other
  fiery chilli paste)

To serve:
drizzle of Buffalo Sauce (page 79)
  or other hot sauce
1 soft white hot dog roll
2–3 chillies, finely sliced (the
variety you choose will define the
  overall heat)

METHOD

Mix the mayonnaise and chipotle in adobo together to a smooth consistency.

Cook the sausage, as per the method for Loaded Dogs (page 92).

Lay the sausage in the roll, then cover in buffalo sauce.

Spoon over a generous amount of the chipotle mayonnaise.

Top with as many chilli slices as you can balance on top.

Inflict on your chosen victim.

TACOS AL PASTOR

 200–250°C
300–482°F

Serves 4–6

INGREDIENTS

2 pork tenderloins, approx.
 400g/14oz each

For the marinade:
3 garlic cloves, peeled
2–3 peppers from a jar of chipotle
 in adobo
150ml/5fl oz/²/₃ cup pineapple
 juice
1 tbsp cider vinegar
2 tbsp brown sugar
1 tbsp achiote paste
1 tbsp ancho chilli flakes
1 tsp cumin
1 tsp dried oregano
pinch of Maldon sea salt
pinch of freshly ground black
 pepper

To serve:
15cm/6in corn tortillas (you'll need
 2–3 per person)
½ head white cabbage, very
 finely shredded
1 portion of Pineapple and
 Habanero Salsa (page 202)
juice of 1 lime
red chillies, finely sliced
small bunch of coriander, leaves
 picked

Al pastor (meaning 'shepherd style') tacos are the definitive street food of Mexico City. Typically, layers of marinated pork strips are stacked up on a vertical spit or rotisserie (similar to a Middle Eastern shawarma), with the meat being shaved off as it cooks. In fact, it is believed that this method of cooking was introduced to Mexico by Lebanese immigrants back in the 19th century and this led to the awesome fusion of cooking technique and flavours. A massive vertical spit is clearly impossible in a wood oven, but we can recreate the huge flavours and wonderful aromas.

The key ingredient here is achiote. Generally, I've tried to avoid using too many hard-to-find ingredients throughout this book, but this really is essential and, in my view, gives the whole dish its signature flavour and colour. It's made from ground annatto seeds, and you can find it either as a paste – which we'll be using in this recipe – or a ground powder. Try a good online Mexican grocer if you are struggling to get hold of it locally.

I've opted for pork tenderloins here, as they cook quickly and are quite happy tolerating the high heat of a wood oven, but feel free to experiment with different cuts of pork if you fancy. I've used the same marinade on a quartered chicken several times with great success.

The marinade will keep for up to a week in a sealed jar in the fridge, but it also freezes really well if you want to make a bigger batch.

METHOD

Add all the marinade ingredients to a food processor. Blitz to a smooth paste.

Place the tenderloins in a dish and smother in the marinade. Cover and set aside in the fridge for a few hours.

Preheat a cast-iron baking tray. Once hot, carefully place the tenderloins on the tray.

Slide into the oven and cook for 10–15 minutes, turning regularly until the internal temperature of the meat hits 65°C/149°F.

Set the pork aside to rest.

Heat your tacos in the oven for a few seconds on each side, then wrap in a clean tea towel to keep warm and soft.

Slice the pork as thinly as possible.

Build your tacos as follows: tortilla, white cabbage, pork, pineapple salsa, squeeze of lime juice, chilli and coriander leaves.

TANDOORI-STYLE CHICKEN

RECIPE BY MARCUS BAWDON

150–200°C
300–400°F

Serves 2

INGREDIENTS

4–6 bone-in, skin-on chicken
 thighs
2 lemon or lime wedges

For the marinade:
3 tbsp natural yoghurt
2 tsp homemade or shop-bought
 tandoori spice mix
pinch of salt and pepper
juice of ½ lime or lemon

To serve:
cooked white rice
coriander leaves

The spiced marinade does all the work in this tandoori-style recipe and the wood-fired oven gives a wonderful flavour.

METHOD

Mix up the tandoori marinade by stirring all the marinade ingredients together in a large bowl.

Add the chicken thighs, stir and leave in the fridge for 1–2 hours.

Place the chicken and citrus fruit wedges in a cast-iron skillet.

Cook for around 20 minutes, or until the skin is crispy and slightly charred, and the chicken is cooked through, ensuring that it hits an internal temperature of 74°C/165°F.

Serve with white rice, coriander and the charred citrus fruit squeezed over the top.

Marcus is well known throughout the live-fire cooking world for his cookbooks, outdoor cookery website Country Woodsmoke, and newly launched UK BBQ School in Devon, England. A cook with an ever-increasing quiver of live-fire cooking techniques, Marcus is consultant editor of BBQ magazine.
@countrywoodsmoke

SIMPLE
SEAFOOD

MUSSELS GRATIN

**250–330°C
482–626°F**

Serves 4 as a side or 2 as a main

INGREDIENTS

500g/1lb 2oz fresh mussels,
  scrubbed clean and beards
  removed
50ml/2fl oz/scant ¼ cup white
  wine
50g/1¾oz/¾ cup breadcrumbs
30g/1oz/¼ cup Parmesan, finely
  grated
2 garlic cloves, crushed (or 2 tsp
  garlic puree)
small bunch of flat-leaf parsley
2 tbsp extra virgin olive oil
pinch of salt

I simply adore this classic Italian dish. It makes a great starter to share, especially if you are having fish for a main course. Or, as a delicious light lunch in the sunshine with an ice-cold glass of white wine.

It's a two-stage cooking process, so the dish can easily be prepared in advance of guests arriving – top with the breadcrumb mix, then slip the mussels into the oven just before serving.

METHOD

Preheat a cast-iron dish in the oven. Once hot, add the cleaned mussels along with the white wine.

Put a lid on the dish or tightly seal with foil.

Slide the dish into the oven for 4–5 minutes, shaking occasionally until all the mussels have opened.

Remove from the oven. Allow to cool enough to handle, then discard any mussels that have not opened.

In a food processor, blitz the breadcrumbs, Parmesan, garlic and parsley until very finely chopped. Add the olive oil and blitz again until loosely combined.

Remove and discard the upper shell from each mussel.

Sprinkle the moist breadcrumb mix onto each mussel, filling the empty space around the meat and a little over the top. Don't press the mixture down – we want this loose and crumbly, so just let the mixture drop on top.

Lay the mussels on a baking tray and slide back into the oven for 5–6 minutes until golden brown and steaming hot.

TIGER PRAWNS WRAPPED IN BACON

200–250°C
300–482°F

Makes 8

INGREDIENTS

8 tiger prawns (or other large
  prawns), peeled and deveined
8 rashers of thin-cut, dry-cured,
  streaky bacon
pinch of Old Bay seasoning (or
  your favourite seasoning/rub)

In the majority of cases, taking something delicious and wrapping it in bacon usually makes it even tastier – and this simple dish is no exception. This recipe calls for particularly large prawns and dry-aged, thinly sliced streaky bacon. It's important that the bacon has been sliced thinly, as we don't want the prawn to overcook while the bacon crisps up.

If you buy shell-on prawns, carefully remove the shell first but leave the little tail section in place to use as a handle while eating. To remove the vein, use a sharp paring knife and gently score down the whole length of the back of the prawn and scrape or tug the black line out.

I like to add a little seasoning and, here, I'm using a sprinkling of Old Bay. I love to use this seasoning but feel free to experiment – Cajun or Creole seasonings would work well here, or a classic barbecue-style rub with salt, black pepper, paprika and garlic powder. Be sparing with anything too salty, as the bacon will bring enough salt to this party. We're wrapping the bacon along the whole length of the prawn so that every single bite offers the perfect combo.

You can prep these several hours or even a day in advance to make a quick and easy, tasty snack for guests.

METHOD

Take one rasher of bacon and one prawn and, starting at one end, carefully and tightly wrap the bacon all the way along, overlapping slightly at each turn making sure there aren't any loose or baggy sections that may unravel during cooking.

Place the bacon wrapped prawns on a plate or tray, cover in cling film and place in the fridge for 30 minutes (or longer if you wish). This firms up the bacon and helps it 'set' in place before you cook.

After 30 minutes, season the bacon with a sprinkling of Old Bay.

Place on a cooking tray and slide into the oven for 4–5 minutes.

Once the top has crisped up nicely, carefully flip all the prawns and slide back into the oven for a few more minutes until the bacon is just right on both sides.

COD LOIN
WITH WHITE WINE, CAPERS & SAMPHIRE

A great example of a lovely restaurant-style dish that can be cooked in your wood oven. I often cook this for friends and it's quite a showstopper. But, as you'll see from the ingredients and cooking method, it's a really easy dish to make.

As with all fish, make sure it's as fresh as possible. The flesh should be firm with no signs of it starting to mush around the edges. And it should smell of the sea, not fish!

Go easy with the seasoning, as the samphire and capers are already salty.

**200–250°C
300–482°F**

Serves 2

INGREDIENTS

2 cod loins
olive oil
125ml/4fl oz/½ cup white wine
handful of samphire
1 tbsp capers
knob of butter
salt and freshly ground black
 pepper

METHOD

Preheat a cast-iron dish or pan.

Dry the fish, lightly coat with oil and season lightly with salt and pepper.

Gently lay the fish down in the pan and slide back into the oven.

When the fish is almost cooked through (the internal temperature should be around 60°C/140°F), splash in the wine and add the samphire and capers.

When the wine has reduced by half, remove the fish and samphire and set aside on a serving platter.

Add the butter to the hot pan. Whisk to emulsify, then pour over the fish.

GRILLED SWORDFISH
WITH SALMORIGLIO

250–330°C
482–626°F

Serves 2

INGREDIENTS

2 swordfish steaks, approx.
 3–4cm/1¼–1½in thick
small bunch of flat-leaf parsley,
 finely chopped

For the salmoriglio:
juice and zest of 1 lemon
approx. 100ml/3½fl oz/scant
 ½ cup olive oil, plus extra for
 brushing
1 garlic clove, finely chopped (or
 1 tsp garlic puree)
small bunch of oregano, finely
 chopped
generous pinch of Maldon sea salt
freshly ground black pepper

To serve:
seasonal vegetables

If you close your eyes and breathe in the aroma of this dish, you'll be transported to a little beachside café, basking in the warmth of the Sicilian or Calabrian sunshine. It is Southern Italy on a plate.

Salmoriglio is an ancient Sicilian dressing made from lemons and herbs. Versions can be found all over the island as well as into mainland Italy and Greece.

You can swap the fish out for tuna or monkfish if you prefer, but it needs to be a fairly meaty fish to stand up to the powerful flavours of the salmoriglio. I also cook butterflied chicken breasts the same way – equally delicious!

As with any fish dish, freshness is key. Fresh swordfish should be clean and white, with a slightly briny oceanic smell. It should not smell of fish! You may see a brown or red streak in the meat, which is absolutely fine.

Think of cooking swordfish or tuna like cooking steak. Medium rare is great and overcooking will lead to dry fish. We're aiming for an internal temperature of 60°C/140°F. Also, as with steak, we want to find nice thick slices to give us the chance to build up a good sear on each side without overcooking the centre.

METHOD

Preheat a cast-iron skillet in the oven.

In a small bowl, mix together the juice and zest of the lemon, the olive oil, the garlic, the oregano, the salt and the pepper.

Brush each swordfish steak with olive oil. Gently lay them into the preheated skillet and slide into the oven.

After 2–3 minutes, carefully flip the swordfish steaks over.

Cook for a further 2–3 minutes, or until the internal temperature hits 60°C/140°F.

Remove the skillet from the oven. While the fish is still smoking hot, brush generously with half the salmoriglio and garnish with parsley.

Transfer to a serving platter and serve with a small bowl of the remaining salmoriglio and your favourite seasonal veg.

MACKEREL
WITH GINGER, LIME & SPRING ONIONS

Mackerel is an abundant, tasty fish and very easy on the pocket. Its robustness, in terms of both flavour and texture, means it stands up well to being cooked on a grill or in a wood oven. This is a great dish to brighten up the fish and add a little zing to your day.

I've used mackerel fillets here, but do feel free to use whole mackerel (gutted, of course), sliced into 2.5cm (1in) thick rounds, if you prefer. The cooking method is the same.

METHOD

Preheat a cast-iron baking tray.

Whisk the dressing ingredients together in a small bowl and set aside.

Add a drizzle of oil to the hot tray. Carefully lay the mackerel onto the tray, skin side down.

Slide the tray into the oven and roast until the mackerel is cooked through (or reaches an internal temperature of 60°C/140°F).

Carefully place the fish on a serving platter and generously spoon over the dressing.

Add a pile of spring onions to each fillet and serve.

 250–330°C
482–626°F

Serves 2

INGREDIENTS

olive oil, for cooking
3 mackerel fillets, skin on
3–4 spring onions, sliced into
  5mm/¼in rounds

For the dressing:
1 red chilli, finely chopped
1 garlic clove, finely chopped
½ thumb-sized piece of root
  ginger, grated
zest and juice of 1 lime
2 tbsp white wine vinegar
2 tbsp olive oil
pinch of Maldon sea salt

PANCETTA-WRAPPED COD

If you've flipped through a few pages of this book already (or read any of my other books for that matter), you'll know that I am all in favour of adding bacon to recipes, wherever possible, and here is a beautiful example to illustrate the premise.

Yes, skillet-roasted cod is lovely in its own right, but what happens if you add the wonderful flavour of bacon into the mix, too? Well, it's absolutely lip-smackingly delicious. The crispy bacon outside, the tender and succulent fish, the way the saltiness of the bacon seasons the fish as it cooks – it's just fabulous. We're using pancetta in this recipe, a very thinly cut Italian-style bacon. The lightness and crispness work perfectly.

If you are short of time, pick up a sachet of the pre-cooked puy or green lentils from the supermarket. There are some really good ones out there now.

150–200°C
300–400°F

Serves 2

INGREDIENTS

rapeseed oil, for cooking
2 cod loins (approx. 150g/5½oz
 each)
6 slices of pancetta
6 sage or basil leaves (optional)
6–8 cherry tomatoes, on the vine

For the lentils:
½ onion, very finely diced
½ carrot, very finely diced
½ stick celery, very finely diced
3–4 sprigs of thyme, leaves picked
1 tbsp tomato puree
100ml/3½fl oz/scant ½ cup
 white wine
250g/9oz/scant 1½ cups cooked
 puy or green lentils

To serve:
few sprigs of parsley, chopped

METHOD

Add a splash of oil to a cast-iron dish. Add the onion, carrot and celery and sauté until softened.

Add the thyme and tomato purée and continue to cook for 1 minute.

Add the wine and lentils and stir well until the liquid has evaporated. Set aside somewhere warm while you cook the fish.

Slide a cast-iron dish into the oven to preheat.

Lay three slices of pancetta on a chopping board next to each other. You can place a few fresh sage or basil leaves onto the pancetta at this point, if you like.

Place the fish on top and fold the pancetta around each side to join on top of the fillet.

Repeat for the other loin.

Hold a piece of kitchen paper with tongs and use to wipe the hot dish with little oil, then carefully place the fish into the dish, with the join in the pancetta underneath.

After about 5 minutes, add the cherry tomatoes to the pan to roast a little.

Cook for a further 5 minutes or so until the internal temperature of the fish hits 60°C/140°F and the pancetta has crisped up.

Spoon the lentils into a serving bowl, gently place the fish on top and the tomatoes along the side.

Garnish with parsley.

PUGLIAN-STYLE SEA BREAM

Sea bream is one of the most prolific fish in the food markets of Europe. Known as dorada in Spain, orata in Italy, dorade in France and dourada in Portugal, you'll see it on the menu of every beachside eatery you visit. Sea bream is competitively priced, easy to prep and cook, and delicious to eat.

We often stay in Puglia, on the very 'heel' of Italy, where the Ionian and Adriatic Seas meet and the waters are abundant with all kinds of amazing seafood, including orata. This is quite a traditional Pugliese way to cook the dish and, of course, would originally have been cooked in a wood-fired oven!

Ideally, use a mandoline to slice the potato and fennel – it needs to be super thin, so that it cooks quickly. This recipe is really good served with Grilled Peppers (page 68).

200–250°C
300–482°F

Serves 2

INGREDIENTS

1–2 Desiree (or other waxy)
  potatoes, scrubbed or peeled
1 fennel bulb
olive oil
125ml/4fl oz/½ cup white wine
1 whole sea bream, scaled,
  gutted and cleaned
1 garlic clove, thinly sliced
½ lemon, sliced into rounds
2–3 sprigs of oregano
Maldon sea salt
freshly ground black pepper

METHOD

Thinly slice the potatoes and fennel. Layer at the bottom of a cast-iron baking dish to a depth of around 1.5cm (⁵/₈in).

Season with sea salt and pepper.

Drizzle with olive oil and add the wine.

Slide the tray into the oven to give the vegetables a head start while you prepare the fish.

Make 3 diagonal cuts, about 1cm (½in) deep, in each side of the fish.

Open up the cavity and stuff with the garlic, lemon, oregano and a sprinkle of salt and pepper.

Take the potatoes and fennel out of the oven (they should have just started to soften) and lay the fish on top.

The fish should be cooked after about 15–20 minutes, but check by gently tugging at the dorsal fin – if it comes away cleanly and easily the fish is done. If you are cooking to an internal temperature, then 60–65°C/140–149°F is a good target.

Transfer the fish to a serving platter or just place the baking tray directly on a trivet in the centre of the table.

PONZU TROUT

Ponzu is a store-cupboard essential in our house. It's a citrus-flavoured soy sauce, which gives you all the deep umami flavour associated with soy, but also a hit of bright tanginess from the ponzu. It works incredibly well with fish, as you will find out when you cook this recipe!

You can substitute the trout for most other types of fish. Sea bass, bream and salmon fillets all work very well, but I love the light delicateness of trout and, as the fillets are so thin, it cooks in just a few minutes. When it comes to the chilli, you can choose any kind you like, depending on the level of heat you enjoy.

Most major supermarkets now sell furikake and togarashi, but they are also available from Asian supermarkets.

**200–250°C
300–482°F**

Serves 2–3

INGREDIENTS

2 rainbow or brown trout fillets,
  skin on, approx. 100g/3½oz each
150ml/5fl oz/⅔ cup ponzu sauce
juice of 1 lime
thumb-sized piece of root ginger,
  finely grated
1 red chilli, finely diced

To serve:
furikake seaweed flakes
shichimi togarashi seasoning
coriander leaves

METHOD

In a dish large enough to hold the trout, mix together the ponzu, lime juice, ginger and chilli.

Add the fish to the dish and make sure it is well coated in the marinade.

Leave to marinate for at least half an hour in the fridge.

Preheat a cast-iron tray in the oven. Add the fish to the tray, placing it skin side down. Set the leftover marinade aside.

Transfer the tray to the oven and cook until the internal temperature of the fish reaches 50°C/122°F.

Carefully add a tablespoon or so of the leftover marinade to each fillet, then slide back into the oven until the internal temperature reaches 60°C/140°F.

Transfer to a serving platter and garnish with a sprinkle of furikake, shichimi togarashi and coriander.

GARLIC BUTTER COCKLES

This is a recipe I have cooked for years using clams, but I recently decided to play around with good old-fashioned cockles instead. The cockle is a big brother to the clam but equally sweet and succulent.

You'll need a baking tray or dish that's at least 2.5cm (1in) deep and also something to cover the dish as the cockles steam open – you can just use foil for this, if that's all you have that fits.

I always soak cockles or clams for at least three to four hours (or overnight) in a big bowl of salty cold water before cooking them. This helps purge them of any residual sand.

**250–330°C
482–626°F**

Serves 4

INGREDIENTS

500g/1lb 2oz cockles (or clams)
4 garlic cloves, crushed
125ml/4fl oz/½ cup white wine
50g/1¾oz/¼ cup butter
small bunch of flat-leaf parsley,
 finely chopped

To serve:
1 portion of Toasted Bread
(page 52)

METHOD

Preheat a cast-iron baking tray or dish.

Add the cockles, along with the garlic and the wine.

Cover and slide into the oven for 4–5 minutes.

Check the cockles have all opened. If not, return to the oven for a few more minutes.

Remove from the oven and discard any cockles that remain closed.

Add the butter and mix well into the wine broth.

Add the parsley and mix well.

Tip into a serving dish. Mop up all the juices with some freshly made toasted bread.

MISO COD RAMEN

**150–200°C
300–400°F**

Serves 2

INGREDIENTS

2 x 150–180g/5½–6oz skinless
 cod loins
ramen noodle kit (to serve 2)
olive oil
approx. 100g/3½oz samphire (or
 finely shredded white cabbage)
salt and freshly ground black
 pepper

For the glaze:
1½ tbsp honey
1½ tbsp soy sauce
1½ tbsp mirin (or dry sherry)
3 tbsp miso paste

To serve:
1 red chilli, thinly sliced
small bunch of coriander, leaves
 picked
juice of 1 lime
aonori seaweed flakes

This dish is so fresh with lime and an ozone hit of the ocean, yet at the same time it's full of rich, satisfying umami flavours. Plus, the woodsmoke from the oven adds an extra layer of complexity and flavour.

Monkfish tail fillets would make a good alternative to cod, but you can use any fresh fish of your choosing. If you can't get hold of mirin for the glaze, use a dry sherry instead.

METHOD

A few hours before you plan to eat, mix together the glaze ingredients in a small bowl. Place the fish and the glaze mixture into a ziplock bag, squeeze out the air, then seal and place in the fridge.

Set up your oven to a medium heat.

Following the ramen noodle kit instructions, prepare the ramen broth and leave on a very gentle simmer until you are ready to use.

Preheat a cast-iron skillet. Brush the fish with a little oil and season. Place the fish in the skillet and cook for a few minutes until slightly charred and cooked through. (Resist the temptation to move it around as it cooks.)

When the fish is cooked, set aside and loosely cover with foil to keep it warm.

Plunge the samphire into the simmering broth for 60 seconds to soften. Remove and plunge into a bowl of ice-cold water. Leave for a few minutes, then drain and set aside.

Cook the noodles, following the packet instructions, then transfer to 2 bowls, along with the broth, samphire and cod fillets.

Garnish with chilli, coriander leaves, a squeeze of lime juice and a sprinkle of aonori seaweed flakes.

FAMILY
FEASTS

PARMIGIANA

Aubergines can divide people, and I understand that, but parmigiana is magnificent. It's usually layered up in a big dish, similar to lasagne, but I really like to build it into individual towers of mozzarella and lovely pizza sauce, with a melty cheesy hat. It's also surprisingly good cold, so always make extra so you have some stashed in the fridge for the next day.

METHOD

Preheat a cast-iron baking dish or tray.

Slice the aubergine into 1–1.5cm (½ –⁵/₈in) thick rounds

Drizzle both sides with oil and cook until softened and starting to char.

Remove from the oven and place on a cold cast-iron baking tray.

Top each aubergine slice with a basil leaf or two, a drizzle of pizza sauce, a slice of mozzarella and a pinch of Parmesan.

Slide into the oven until piping hot and the cheese has melted.

**250–330°C
482–626°F**

Serves 2

INGREDIENTS

oil, for cooking
1 aubergine
200g/7oz/1 cup pizza sauce or
 passata
1 buffalo mozzarella, sliced
small handful of grated Parmesan
small bunch of basil, leaves picked

THE PERFECT STEAK

250–330°C
482–626°F

Serves 2–4

INGREDIENTS

2 thick-cut (approx. 3cm/1¼in)
 T-bone, sirloin or rib-eye steaks
olive oil
large knob of butter
2–3 sprigs of rosemary
3 garlic cloves, whole and
 unpeeled
Maldon sea salt and freshly
 ground black pepper

I've always preferred a steak cooked in a heavy, flat-bottomed cast-iron skillet to one cooked on the grill bars of a barbecue. You get a much better and more even sear. The steak retains more moisture, you have more control over the cooking and it's easy to add an extra hit of flavour with some butter and herbs in the pan.

It's always best to choose a thicker, but small-sized steak than a larger flat one. You need the thickness to allow a good sear to build up before the steak gets overdone.

METHOD

Place a cast-iron skillet in the oven until it is screaming hot.

Lightly oil the steaks and season generously with salt and black pepper.

Gently lay the steaks down into the pan and slide back into the oven. Flip after 2–3 minutes, then add the butter to the pan along with the rosemary and garlic.

Cook for a few more minutes, basting the meat with a spoon as you go. Continue to baste and flip until you reach your desired done-ness (see chart below).

Remove steaks from the pan onto a plate, tip over the juices from the pan and rest under tented foil for 10 minutes.

Slice onto a serving plate and pour over the resting juices.

Sprinkle with sea salt.

Steak Cooking Guide

Degree of done-ness	Internal temperature
Rare	52°C/125.6°F
Medium rare	55°C/131°F
Medium	62°C/143.6°F
Well done	68+°C/154.4+°F

TAGLIATA

For a bright, summery change to your usual way of serving steak, give tagliata a try. In addition to your cooked steaks, you'll need a large handful of rocket, a block of Parmesan, a lemon, olive oil and sea salt.

It's super simple to prepare. First, arrange the rocket on a serving platter or large plate, then thinly slice the steak and arrange on top of the rocket. Shave over some Parmesan. Drizzle with lemon juice and olive oil. Finish with a sprinkle of sea salt.

HAWAIIAN YAKITORI CHICKEN

**200–250°C
300–482°F**

Serves 2–3

INGREDIENTS

oil, for greasing
2 large chicken breasts, approx.
 400g/14oz each, cut into
 2cm/¾in cubes
few glugs of teriyaki sauce
1 red pepper
1 green pepper
½ fresh pineapple
sesame seeds

You'll also need:
metal skewers

Yakitori is Japanese skewered meat (usually chicken or pork) grilled over fire. The wood-fired oven does an amazing job of replicating the searing heat usually associated with cooking this dish. The pineapple and peppers add a lovely hit of colour and give a delicious sweet, fresh and juicy angle. This is a family favourite on heavy rotation in our house and one the kids can easily help to prepare.

You'll need some decent skewers. I like to use flattened metal ones in the wood oven as the usual bamboo or wooden ones catch fire too easily. The flattening also helps stop the food rotating as you turn it.

METHOD

Place the chicken in a bowl and add the teriyaki sauce. Stir until well coated. Set aside in the fridge while you prepare the rest of the ingredients.

Deseed the peppers, then cut into 2cm (¾in) squares.

Peel and core the pineapple, then cut into 2cm (¾in) cubes.

Take your skewers and thread on a piece of chicken. Next, add a piece of pepper, followed by another piece of chicken, then a pineapple cube.

Continue in this manner until you've filled your skewers.

Lightly wipe over a baking tray with oil and then preheat in the oven.

Place the skewers on the tray and slide into the oven.

Cook, turning regularly, until almost cooked through, then add a sprinkle of sesame seeds.

Continue cooking until the chicken reaches 75°C/167°F in the thickest part – this should take around 8 minutes in total.

PICANHA

**200–250°C
300–482°F**

Serves 6

INGREDIENTS

1 whole picanha, approx.
 1–1.5kg/2lb 4oz–3lb 5oz
olive oil
Maldon sea salt and freshly
 ground black pepper (or your
 favourite beef rub – make sure
 it's sugar free)
100g/3½oz/scant ½ cup butter
4–5 garlic cloves
sprig of rosemary

To serve:
Maldon sea salt
Chimichurri (page 199)

If there was ever a cut of meat perfectly suited to cooking over fire, then it's the picanha. A traditional South American 'churrasco' grill cut, it's one of the tastiest pieces of beef you will find, and one that many grill masters would name as their favourite. It's taken from the top of the rump, so has all the flavour associated with rump steaks yet is a fairly underused muscle so remains beautifully tender. A whole picanha (1–1.5kg/2lb 4oz–3lb 5oz) is a great size to share, easy to cook, great value and a real showstopper.

This is not a cut of meat commonly found in your local supermarket, but it is starting to pop up on the counters of good independent butchers up and down the country. It's always a good idea to give your butcher a heads-up a few days in advance when you are planning to cook more unusual cuts.

Often cut thickly and loaded onto skewers before cooking, I prefer to start things off by keeping the joint whole, gently rendering out some of the thick layer of fat, before slicing and returning to the fire to sear the individual pieces.

METHOD

Preheat a cast-iron tray.

Remove the picanha from the fridge, remove all packaging and pat the meat dry. Allow it to reach room temperature.

With a sharp knife, score the layer of fat every 1cm (½in) or so.

Rub lightly with oil and then generously season with sea salt and black pepper.

Place the picanha on the preheated tray, fat-side up, and slide it into the oven to start rendering the fat.

Once the fat has started to crisp up, remove from the heat and cut lengthways into three thick slices (cutting with the grain not across it), to give you three long steaks of roughly similar thickness and width.

Return each piece back to the heat. Turn the meat regularly for an all-over sear, then, about 5 minutes before your meat has reached your preferred level of done-ness, add the butter, garlic and rosemary to the tray and baste the meat regularly, turning it often in the delicious meaty, buttery, aromatic juices.

Once the steaks are done, remove from the heat and allow to rest, uncovered, for 10–15 minutes.

Slice each steak across the grain into 0.5–1cm (¼–½in) rounds, pour over the remaining pan juices, sprinkle with sea salt and serve with chimichurri.

BRITISH TOAD-IN-THE-HOLE

200–250°C
300–482°F

Serves 4

INGREDIENTS

oil, for greasing
4 large eggs
120g/4¼oz/1 level cup plain flour
250ml/9fl oz/1 level cup milk
8 sausages or 12 chipolatas

To serve:
mashed potato
onion gravy

A British classic! And perfect for cooking in a wood oven. This is my go-to batter recipe that can also be used for Yorkshire puddings (which, incidentally, are also magnificent cooked in the wood oven).

I like to use a measuring jug to mix all the ingredients together, adding each one up to the level of the next 250ml (9fl oz) increment. It saves faffing about with scales. Alternatively, you can measure the ingredients into a US measuring cup, using 1 level cup of each.

This recipe makes one large toad-in-the-hole or 12 individual Yorkshire puddings in a muffin tray.

METHOD

Gently mix all the ingredients together until just combined. (Don't overmix the batter, or the gluten in the flour will activate too much and your Yorkshire pudding will not rise.)

Place the batter mix in the fridge for at least 30 minutes, but ideally a couple of hours.

Preheat a cast-iron tray (ideally, a round one so you can spin it as it cooks).

Lightly oil the tray. Add the sausages and slide back into the oven.

Turn the sausages every few minutes until browned all over. (They do not need to be cooked through in the middle at this point.)

Carefully pour in the batter and return the dish to the oven.

Rotate the pan every 5 minutes or so, until the batter has puffed up and turned a lovely golden brown.

Insert a toothpick into the batter to check it is cooked all the way through (the toothpick should come out clean).

Slice and serve with a big pile of mashed potato and lashings of onion gravy.

ALBONDIGAS

A classic Spanish tapas, albondigas are rich with smoked paprika and delicious washed down with a glass of Rioja in the sunshine. Dishes like this are made for wood ovens, with everything happening in just one pan, and these meatballs are quick, easy and moreish.

This recipe will make around 16 small meatballs. They should be bite-size.

METHOD

Tear up the white bread into 1cm (½in) chunks and add to a mixing bowl.

Add the milk and mix it all around.

Add the pork mince, beef mince, ½ tsp smoked paprika, garlic, beaten egg, half the chopped parsley and a pinch of salt and pepper.

Mix everything together and form into 16 small meatballs.

Preheat a skillet in the oven, slosh in a glug of oil and carefully add the meatballs.

Allow to brown, moving around a little as they start to sear.

When the meatballs are cooked (this should take around 8–10 minutes), remove them from the skillet and set aside.

Add the red wine to the pan along with the chopped tomatoes, ½ tsp smoked paprika and the chilli.

Allow to simmer until reduced by about half, stirring to deglaze the pan. Add the meatballs back to the pan and allow to heat through.

Garnish with the rest of the parsley and serve straight from the pan.

**200–250°C
300–482°F**

Makes 16

INGREDIENTS

rapeseed oil, for cooking

2 slices of white bread

6 tbsp milk

200g/7oz pork mince

200g/7oz beef mince

1 tsp smoked paprika

1 garlic clove, crushed

1 egg, beaten

small handful of parsley, finely
 chopped

175ml/6fl oz/¾ cup light Spanish
 red wine

200g/7oz/1 cup chopped
 tomatoes

1 red chilli, finely sliced

salt and pepper

SLOW-COOKED SHOULDER OF LAMB
ON BOULANGÈRE POTATOES

**90–150°C
194–300°F**

Serves 6

INGREDIENTS

extra virgin olive oil
1 onion, thinly sliced
6 large floury potatoes, thinly
  sliced (approx. 2–3mm/1/16–1/8in
  thick)
5–6 sprigs of fresh thyme, woody
  stalks removed
1.5kg/3lb 5oz lamb shoulder on
  the bone
Maldon sea salt and freshly
  ground black pepper
500ml/18fl oz/2 cups chicken
  stock
3–4 garlic cloves, whole and
  unpeeled
few sprigs of rosemary

To serve:
seasonal vegetables

This is a fabulous Sunday celebration dish that can be popped in a low oven first thing in the morning and be ready for a delicious late lunch, filling the house with its glorious aroma as it cooks.

Lamb shoulder is an incredibly forgiving cut. It's very hard to overcook, so you can literally stick it in the oven and forget about it. The meat should fall apart with the slightest pressure.

Desiree are a good choice for boulangère potatoes, which take their name from the French term for 'baker' (anything 'boulangère' would have traditionally been cooked in a baker's oven). Boulangère potatoes are thinly sliced, then cooked in a little stock and herbs.

This is a recipe for a bigger oven that can hold a low and slow temperature for several hours. French beans, savoy cabbage or heavily buttered and peppered spring greens will all work well as side dishes.

METHOD

In a bowl, mix together the sliced onions and potatoes with a little olive oil and a generous sprinkling of thyme.

Rub the lamb with olive oil and liberally season with salt and pepper.

Evenly layer the potato and onion mix in the bottom of a baking tray, then place the lamb on top.

Pour the chicken stock over the potatoes.

Scatter over the garlic and rosemary.

Slide into the oven for 4–5 hours, or until the lamb is fall-apart tender and the potatoes are crispy on top and soft inside. If the lamb starts to catch, loosely cover with foil.

Remove from the oven and allow to rest uncovered for 15 minutes while you prepare the accompanying veg.

Set the tray on a wooden board in the middle of the table and let everyone help themselves.

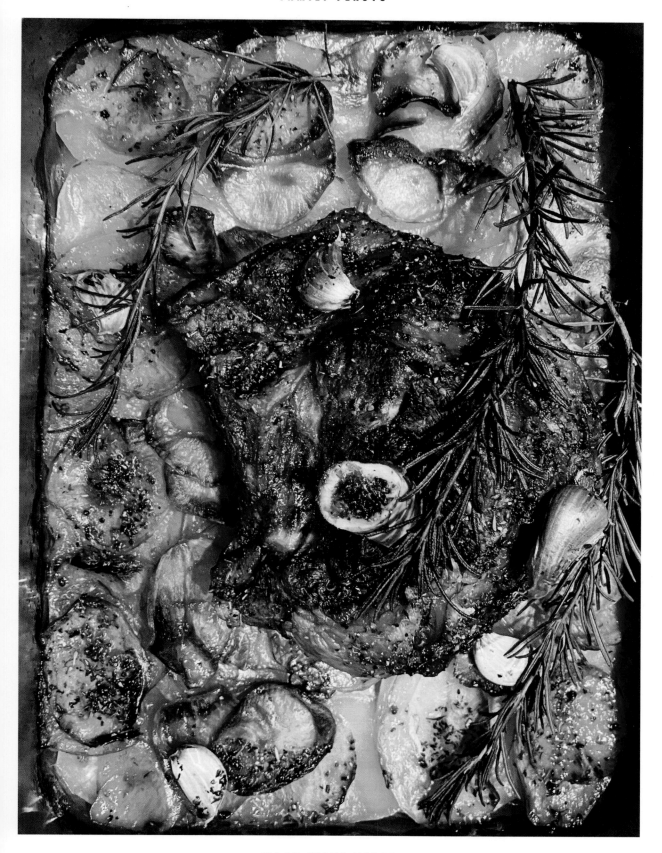

CELERIAC SHAWARMA
WITH POMEGRANATE & MINT

 **150–200°C
300–400°F**

Serves 6

INGREDIENTS

1 celeriac
1–2 tbsp shawarma paste
olive oil

For the dressing:
2 tbsp tahini
4 tbsp natural yoghurt
2 tbsp lemon juice
½ tsp salt
1 garlic clove, crushed (or 1 tsp
 garlic puree)

To serve:
Very Good Flatbreads (page 42),
 warmed briefly in the oven
iceberg lettuce, thinly shredded
1 tomato, finely diced
¼ cucumber, finely diced
natural yoghurt
hot chilli sauce (optional)
pomegranate seeds
bunch of mint, roughly chopped
pickled chilli peppers (Tatli Biber)

Inspired by the famous Middle Eastern street food, shawarma, this flavour-packed dish swaps out the thinly sliced meat for celeriac, so it's perfect for vegetarians and vegans.

Popular the world over, shawarma is usually made from thin slices of meat that are stacked on top of each other on a long skewer and then grilled. As the outer layers become cooked, the meat is shaved off into wraps, while the meat continues to rotate and cook. We're not spinning anything here, but we are replicating the highly spiced thin shavings of meat, just using celeriac instead!

METHOD

Mix the dressing ingredients together in a small bowl. Set aside.

Peel the celeriac.

Slice the celeriac in half and then thinly slice each half into 2–3mm (1/16–1/8in) slices.

Place the slices in a large bowl and add the shawarma paste along with a generous glug of olive oil.

Mix well until all the celeriac pieces are evenly coated.

Spread the celeriac out on a baking tray and cook for 5–10 minutes until tender.

Layer up your shawarmas as follows:
Flatbread
Lettuce, tomato and cucumber
Celeriac
Tahini dressing
Drizzle of yoghurt
Splash of chilli sauce (optional)
Sprinkle of pomegranate seeds and mint.

Serve with pickled chilli peppers.

FLANK STEAK
WITH PIMENTÓN OIL

Flank is a highly underrated cut of meat. It is flavour-packed and, when cooked well, is every bit as juicy and tender as a ribeye or sirloin. It's crucial not to cook this past medium-rare or it will become tough. It's also important to give it a good long rest to allow the juices to redistribute and the meat to relax.

You'll notice a very wide and obvious grain on this steak. When serving, slice the meat across the grain for ultimate tenderness. I love to eat this with Grilled Peppers (page 68).

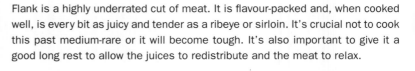

250–330°C
482–626°F

Serves 4

INGREDIENTS

rapeseed oil, for cooking
1 whole flank steak, approx.
 800g/1lb 12oz
Maldon sea salt

To serve:
1 portion of Pimentón Oil
 (page 205)

METHOD

Preheat a cast-iron skillet.

Rub the steak all over with oil and then give it a generous seasoning with sea salt.

Carefully place the steak into the skillet and slide back into the oven.

After 2–3 minutes, flip the steak over and return to the oven.

Keep flipping the steak every few minutes, until it hits 48°C/118°F internally.

Remove from the oven and rest for a good 10 minutes.

Slice against the grain and drizzle with pimentón oil, then finish with a sprinkle of sea salt.

BEERY BRATWURST

This is a German classic! Essentially, we are braising the sausages in the beer and caraway seeds, which keeps them super succulent and incredibly tasty.

Caraway seeds are the real star of the show here and bring an authentic German flavour and aroma to the dish. With a taste that's somewhere between fennel and cumin, caraway is often used to flavour German rye breads and crackers.

When it comes to beer choice, avoid pale ales, as the high level of 'hoppiness' will impart a bitterness to the dish. Instead, choose an English brown ale or a German Doppelbock.

**150–200°C
300–400°F**

Serves 6

INGREDIENTS

butter, for cooking
1 white onion, sliced
1 tbsp caraway seeds
6 German-style bratwurst
 sausages
approx. 250ml/9fl oz/1 cup malty
 dark ale or golden beer
6 hot dog rolls

To serve:
1 portion of Potato Salad (page
 195)
wholegrain or American mustard

METHOD

Melt a generous knob of butter in a skillet. Add the onion and caraway seeds. Place in the oven for a few minutes until the onion softens.

Add the bratwurst and cook until the onions and sausages start to brown (about 6–8 minutes).

Pour in the beer, slide back into the oven and continue to cook until the liquid has reduced by two-thirds.

Split the hot dog rolls open like a book, being careful not to slice all the way through. Add onions and a sausage to each one.

Serve with potato salad and mustard.

CLASSIC BEEF WELLINGTON

This is surely one of the most decadent, celebratory ways to serve beef. Here, the magnificent Wellington is made with the tenderest beef fillet, a duxelles of mushrooms and lovely prosciutto ham.

Beef Wellington has a reputation for being an incredibly technical and difficult dish to prepare. Honestly, it's not, and with the use of a probe thermometer we can make sure the beef is cooked to perfection.

The sheet of pastry will be quite big enough, so rather than buying two packs (which I find gives too thick a crust) I like to lay the pastry out on a well-floured board and roll it a little larger and thinner.

**150–200°C
300–400°F**

Serves 6

INGREDIENTS

olive oil, for cooking
1kg/2lb 4oz beef fillet
300g/10½oz/3 cups chestnut
 mushrooms
1 shallot, very finely chopped
large knob of butter
few sprigs of thyme, leaves picked
small glass of white wine or
 vermouth
12 slices of prosciutto
1 sheet of pre-made puff pastry
2 egg yolks, beaten
1 tbsp nigella seeds
Maldon sea salt

METHOD

Rub the whole beef fillet with oil, then generously season with sea salt.

Preheat a cast-iron skillet. Add the beef and cook until seared all over. This will take around 6–8 minutes. Remove and place in the fridge to rest.

The mushrooms come next. Finely chop all the mushrooms and add to a preheated skillet with the shallot, butter and thyme.

Once the mushrooms have reduced down, add the wine or vermouth.

Continue to cook, stirring often, until all the liquid has evaporated and the mushrooms have a thick paste-like texture.

Lay the prosciutto slices on a board in two rows.

Spread the mushrooms all over the prosciutto, then place the chilled beef fillet on top and carefully wrap the slices around so you have entirely covered the beef.

Place the pastry on a well-floured board, roll out and trim to size. You'll need one rectangular piece that's approx. 2.5cm (1in) wider all the way around than your beef fillet, and a second piece, larger and more square in shape, that's big enough to cover the top and sides.

Place the prosciutto-wrapped beef on the smaller sheet of pastry and brush around the edge with egg yolk.

Gently place the large piece on top, crimping the two sheets together with a fork. Leaving a 2.5cm (1in) margin all the way around, trim off any excess pastry.

Brush the whole thing with egg yolk, then sprinkle the top with nigella seeds and sea salt. Chill the uncooked Wellington for 20 minutes in the fridge.

Place the Wellington on a round baking tray (so you can turn it as it cooks) and slide into the oven. It will take approx. 30 minutes to reach medium-rare, but you can check the exact temperature by inserting a probe thermometer into one end (see page 16).

Allow the Wellington to rest for 10 minutes before slicing and serving.

SIMPLE SKILLET ROAST CHICKEN

As the name suggests, this is a simple yet delicious way to roast a chicken in your wood oven, bringing in a taste of Italy to boot. I like to serve this with a big plate of Grilled Peppers (page 68) and Parmentier Potatoes (page 186).

METHOD

Using poultry shears or very sharp scissors, cut along each side of the backbone, remove and discard.

Flip the chicken over and split down the middle to separate into 2 equal halves.

Trim the wing bones off at the first joint so that just a stub remains.

Lightly rub the chicken with olive oil and season generously with sea salt and black pepper.

Splash a little oil into a large skillet or roasting dish and preheat in the oven.

Carefully place the chicken, meat side down, in the pan.

Squeeze the lemon juice over the chicken and then add the 2 halves to the dish.

Add the oregano and garlic cloves to the dish.

Slide back into the oven and cook for 10–15 minutes, checking and turning the dish often.

Flip the chicken over and carefully baste with the pan juices before sliding back in the oven.

Cook for a further 15 minutes or so, until the chicken is cooked through, basting regularly.

When the chicken is cooked and the skin is nicely browned, remove the chicken from the dish and set aside to rest while you make the sauce.

Add the wine to the pan and slide back in the oven.

When it starts to simmer, remove and, using a spatula, scrape all the brown bits from the bottom of the pan.

Slide back into the oven and cook until the wine has reduced by at least half.

Whisk in the flour until smooth.

Add the stock, whisk together and slide back in the oven until reduced by a third.

Discard the lemon halves, rosemary and garlic. Strain the sauce through a sieve into a clean bowl or jug, then pour over the chicken.

150–200°C
300–400°F

Serves 4

INGREDIENTS

olive oil

1 whole chicken, approx. 1.5kg/
  3lb 5oz

6 garlic cloves, whole and
  unpeeled

1 lemon, halved

4–5 sprigs of oregano

125ml/4fl oz/½ cup white wine

1 tbsp plain flour

250ml/9fl oz/1 cup chicken stock

Maldon sea salt

freshly ground black pepper

BUTTERFLIED LEG OF LAMB

This must be one of my all-time favourites. The trick is to butterfly the leg of lamb, opening it out to a thickness of 2–3cm (¾–1¼in) and then cook it hot and fast, like you would a steak.

You can use this exact same method but with different flavour combinations. Try tandoori or Moroccan paste – even jerk paste works well.

150–200°C
300–400°F

Serves 4–6

INGREDIENTS

1 leg of lamb, approx. 2–2.5kg/4lb 8oz–5lb 8oz

For the wet rub:
3 anchovy fillets
2 garlic cloves, crushed (or 2 tsp garlic puree)
sprig fresh rosemary, leaves picked
1 tbsp capers, drained
1 tbsp Dijon mustard
1½ tbsp olive oil
juice of ½ lemon
Maldon sea salt and freshly ground black pepper

To serve:
seasonal vegetables

METHOD

Locate the bone running through the centre of the joint and, using a sharp knife, carefully run the blade along the bone to remove it. Don't cut all the way through the meat as we want it in one piece.

Open the meat up like a book. You'll find one half is much thicker than the other, so butterfly the thicker side again, unfolding more until the meat is an even thickness. Trim off any excess fat.

Now, make the wet rub. You can roughly chop the ingredients and combine or blitz in a food processor. If the paste is too thick, add a little more olive oil.

Smear the rub all over the leg of lamb, place it on a skillet and slide into the oven. Flip regularly until both sides are golden brown and the internal temperature hits 60°C/140°F.

Set the lamb aside to rest under a piece of loosely tented foil while you prepare and cook the vegetables.

STUFFED CHICKEN THIGHS

**150–200°C
300–400°F**

Serves 3

INGREDIENTS

6 boneless, skinless chicken
  thighs
6 of your favourite sausages
12 rashers of dry-cured, smoked
  streaky bacon
barbecue sauce, for glazing
  (optional)

To serve:
slaw (optional)

You'll also need:
cocktail sticks

Here's a recipe that harks back to my old smokehouse barbecue days. It's a popular dish to sling into a smoker for a couple of hours, but equally delicious cooked in a wood oven.

It's important to cook this gently, though, as the sausage meat stuffing needs time to cook through properly before the bacon burns. We're aiming for crispy bacon, succulent chicken and deliciously seasoned stuffing – a joy with every bite.

Ideally, you'll be able to source skinless, boneless thighs, but if not, carefully remove the skin and the bones (or ask your butcher to do this) so that you have a flat piece of meat to work with.

METHOD

Open out the chicken thighs and lay them on a chopping board with the side that used to have the bone in facing upwards. (As the bacon is salty, there's no need to season them.)

Remove the sausage meat from their casings. Place a strip of sausage meat, about the thickness of your finger, across the width of each chicken thigh where the bone used to be.

Roll the chicken thighs around the sausage meat. It should resemble a fat sausage roll.

Wrap rashers of bacon around each chicken thigh parcel and secure with cocktail sticks, if needed. (You can either wrap them entirely in bacon or leave the ends showing.)

Place on a cast-iron tray and slide into the oven, turning often, until the middle of the pork stuffing hits 75°C/167°F.

If you like, you can coat the parcels with barbecue sauce 5 minutes before the end of their cooking time for an extra layer of flavour.

Serve with slaw on the side.

PORK CHOPS

This recipe is all about showing how one simple ingredient, treated with respect and cooked over a wood fire, can be one of the tastiest things you'll eat. It is absolutely imperative that you seek out the highest quality pork you can find. This is what you are looking for: locally reared, free range, heritage or rare breed; highly marbled meat; dry aged; thick cut and bone in; and at least 2.5cm (1in) of fat around the edge.

You must accept that you will pay more for this meat than you would at the supermarket, but pound for pound, pork still offers tremendous value compared to beef or lamb. Plus, the flavour is incomparable next to most supermarket offerings.

With such a thick layer of fat, the meat will have a tendency to curl or ball up as it cooks. To prevent this from happening, take a very sharp kitchen knife, or Stanley knife, and carefully make vertical slits into the fat every 0.5cm (¼in). This also makes the chops look quite cool, I think.

Serve with French Beans (page 184) and Parmentier Potatoes (page 186), if you like.

200–250°C
300–482°F

Serves 2

INGREDIENTS

rapeseed oil, for cooking
2 thick-cut, bone-in pork chops
Maldon sea salt

METHOD

Make deep scores into the pork fat, as described above.

Preheat a cast-iron baking tray in the oven.

Rub the chops with a little rapeseed oil, then season well with sea salt.

Carefully lay the chops onto the tray and slide back into the oven.

After 4–5 minutes, flip the chops over and cook for a further 2–3 minutes.

Once the internal temperature reaches 60°C/140°F, remove the chops from the tray and rest for 5–6 minutes.

Season again with another generous sprinkle of sea salt.

JERK CHICKEN
WITH MANGO

I love the simplicity of this dish: the big, heady aroma and heat from the jerk spices, which are tempered, refreshed and cooled by the sweet, juicy mango. This is just the kind of food I love to eat.

I put my hands up. I've taken a shortcut and used a shop-bought jerk paste. I've made it from scratch several times and, quite frankly, the decent stuff in the shops is every bit as good, with the added bonus of not having to deal with the fiercely hot scotch bonnet chillies or the fairly lengthy list of component parts.

We're cooking chicken pieces here, but the jerk paste is also terrific on thick-cut pork chops.

 200–250°C
300–482°F

Serves 4

INGREDIENTS

1 whole chicken, approx. 1.5kg/3lb 5oz, cut into pieces
2–3 tbsp jerk paste (I use Walkerswood Traditional Jerk Marinade)
1 ripe mango

METHOD

Smother the chicken in the jerk paste, cover and leave to marinate for a few hours in the fridge.

Place the chicken on a cast-iron baking tray and slide into the oven.

Cook for around 30 minutes, turning often so it gets a nice char all over, or until the temperature of the thickest part reaches 75°C/167°F.

Remove from the oven and rest for 10 minutes.

While the chicken is resting, peel and slice (or dice) a mango.

Arrange on a serving platter for everyone to help themselves.

LAMB & JALAPEÑO SKEWERS

200–250°C
300–482°F

Serves 4

INGREDIENTS

250g/9oz lamb neck fillets, fat
  trimmed and cut into 2.5cm/1in
  pieces
1 tbsp cumin seeds
6 tbsp Greek yoghurt
2 tbsp lemon juice
1 tsp ground coriander
2 tsp dried mint
1 tsp turmeric
10 jalapeño or Padrón peppers

You'll also need:
metal skewers

My friend Dan, who is a terrific chef, came up with this recipe for one of the Live Fire cookery classes we gave. He uses lamb neck fillets, which are very affordable and incredibly tasty, but you can also use lamb leg steaks or loin if you prefer. To help you choose, here's a quick guide to the three cuts:

Neck fillet – most flavour • cheapest to buy • has more chew
Leg steaks – good flavour • more expensive • more tender
Loin fillet – reasonable flavour • most expensive • most tender

I would recommend trying the neck fillets first and if you find them a little tough, move down the scale to the leg. Whichever cut you choose, the recipe remains the same.

Feel free to swap out the jalapeños for Padrón peppers if you don't like too much heat. When it came to photographing this recipe, I used Padrón peppers, as my photographer, Ben, is a bit of a wimp when it comes to chillies!

Don't be tempted to swap the dried mint for fresh mint – dried mint has a very particular flavour, which is crucial for this dish.

METHOD

Preheat a cast-iron skillet. Toast the cumin seeds in the dry pan for a minute or two until their aroma is released.

In a large bowl, mix together the Greek yoghurt, lemon juice, coriander, dried mint, turmeric and the toasted cumin seeds.

Add the meat to the bowl and mix well. Cover and place in the fridge for 2–3 hours.

Remove from the fridge and allow the meat to come up to room temperature. Thread the meat and peppers onto the skewers. Place on a cast-iron baking sheet and slide into the oven.

Turn the skewers regularly until the meat has developed a good colour, is nicely charred and there's no sign of the yoghurt. Once cooked through, the meat will hit an internal temperature of around 60°C/140°F.

MEXICAN CHICKEN

Spatchcocking a chicken is a great way to cook it in your wood-fired oven. The inherent issue with roasting a chicken is that it is a very uneven shape, meaning that it is quite difficult to cook evenly. Invariably, the outer areas cook much faster than the deeper parts of the thighs. By flattening it out, we're making it a much more uniform shape and thickness. Plus, if you have a smaller oven like mine, it makes it far easier to physically get the bird in there.

METHOD

Using poultry shears or a sharp knife, carefully remove the backbone from the chicken and discard.

Open the chicken out like a book and squash it down a little so it lies flat.

Slash the thicker parts of the breast and thigh a few times, then rub with the al pastor marinade.

Cover and leave in the fridge for a couple of hours to marinate.

Place the chicken on a round cast-iron baking tray (so that you can turn it as it cooks) and slide into the oven.

Cook for around 30–40 minutes, turning often, until the internal temperature of the thickest part reaches 75°C/167°F.

Remove from the oven to rest for 10 minutes.

Cut the chicken into pieces, arrange on a serving platter and garnish with lime wedges, sliced chilli and chopped coriander.

Serve with pico de gallo.

**150–200°C
300–400°F**

Serves 4

INGREDIENTS

1 whole chicken (approx. 1.5kg/
  3lb 5oz)
1 portion of al Pastor marinade
  (page 96)

To serve:
1 lime, cut into wedges
2 chillies, sliced
small bunch of coriander, roughly
  chopped
Pico de Gallo (page 200)

BUCATINI

This is a classic Roman pasta dish and you'll find it on virtually every restaurant menu in the city. Italians have incredibly strong views when it comes to which pasta you eat with which sauce, and would never even conceive the notion that this dish could be eaten with anything other than bucatini, a long, hollow spaghetti-like shape. While bucatini is the ideal choice here, you can certainly substitute it with thick spaghetti.

Italians would also declare that this dish must be made with guanciale, which is made from cured pigs' cheeks and is the traditional choice for pasta carbonara. In their opinion, anything other than guanciale would surely ruin the dish! While the cured cheeks are magnificent, unless you live in Italy, they are not readily available, so feel free to use unsmoked pancetta instead.

**150–200°C
300–400°F**

Serves 2

INGREDIENTS

olive oil, for cooking and
 finishing
150g/5½oz/1 cup guanciale or
 unsmoked pancetta, diced
1 red onion, sliced
300–350g/10½–12oz bucatini
3–4 fresh tomatoes, chopped, or
 250g/9oz/1 cup chopped tinned
 tomatoes
1 tsp chilli flakes
splash of red or white wine
 (whichever you happen to have
 open at the time)

METHOD

Add a splash of oil to a cast-iron baking dish, followed by the pancetta.

Slide into the oven and cook until the fat starts to render.

Add the onion to the pan and cook until softened.

Add the tomatoes and chilli flakes and cook for a few minutes.

Pour in the wine. Simmer for 5–10 minutes.

Meanwhile, cook the pasta on the hob, according to the packet instructions.

Mix the pasta and sauce together in a bowl and drizzle with olive oil.

GOAT RAAN
RECIPE BY DAN TOOMBS

90–150°C
194–300°F

Serves 4–6

INGREDIENTS

oil, for cooking
1 x 1.5–2kg/3lb 5oz–4lb 8oz leg of
  goat, surface fat removed
5 garlic cloves, very finely sliced
3 tbsp melted ghee (or unsalted
  butter), for basting
flaky sea salt, to taste

For the marinade:
3 red habanero chillies
5 tbsp crispy fried onions
  (homemade or shop-bought)
3 green bird's eye chillies,
  roughly chopped
1 tbsp ground cumin
1 tbsp ground coriander
1 tbsp garam masala
1 tbsp Kashmiri chilli powder
1 tbsp freshly ground black
  pepper
1 tbsp salt, plus extra to taste
2 tbsp white wine vinegar
4 tbsp lemon juice
4 tbsp garlic and ginger paste
500ml/18fl oz/2 cups Greek
  yoghurt

Raan is traditionally made with goat or mutton. These meats benefit from a lengthy marinating and cooking time, as they are quite tough. You could substitute the goat for a leg of lamb, which would reduce the cooking time to between 2 and 2.5 hours.

I like the sauce spicy and use about three habanero chillies, but feel free to adjust to your own taste.

Serve the raan on its own, or wrap pieces of the meat in hot chapattis or flat breads and top with salad and the sauce.

METHOD

Place all the marinade ingredients, plus 5 tbsp of the yoghurt in a food processor. Blend to a smooth, thick paste. Whisk the paste into the remaining yoghurt. Set aside.

Now it's time to mutilate that goat leg. Make about 10 deep slashes on each side of the leg (it should look like it's been hit by a truck!). Take a sharp knife and make holes all over the meat and fill them with the garlic slices.

Tear off a few large pieces of cling film and layer them in a large, deep baking dish. Place the goat leg on top and pour over the marinade. Rub the marinade all over the meat and into the slits with your hands. Wrap the leg tightly in the cling film and allow to marinate for at least 24 hours or up to 72 hours (the longer the better).

When you're ready to cook, fire up your wood-fired oven. Unwrap the goat leg and scrape off all the marinade. Transfer the marinade to a bowl and keep in the fridge to be used later for the sauce.

Put the goat leg on a cast-iron tray and cover tightly with foil. Place it in the oven and cook for 3 hours, or until fall-apart tender (you should be able to easily pull pieces of meat off the bone).

Remove the foil, return to the oven and cook for 5 minutes per side until nicely charred. Be sure to baste it with the melted ghee! Transfer to a warm platter to rest for about 30 minutes. Season with flaky sea salt.

To make the sauce, pour the retained marinade into a small saucepan and place it on the cooking grate. Stir constantly until the sauce is heated through. Serve alongside the goat.

Californian food blogger Dan, aka The Curry Guy, has spent the best part of 30 years developing and honing his culinary skills, cooking recipes from all over the Indian subcontinent and other parts of Asia. With six cookbooks under his belt, Dan runs curry classes from his Curry Cave in North Yorkshire, UK.
@thecurryguy

SOUTHERN INDIAN CURRY
RECIPE BY MERILEES PARKER

150–200°C
300–400°F

Serves 6

INGREDIENTS

750g/1lb 10oz braising goat
  or lamb shoulder, excess fat
  trimmed and cut into 4cm/1½in
  chunks
2 tbsp coconut oil
12 fresh curry leaves (optional)
750ml/25fl oz/3 cups coconut milk
2 tbsp tamarind paste
1 tbsp garam masala

For the curry paste:

250ml/9fl oz/1 cup coconut cream
bunch of coriander, stalks only
  (leaves reserved)
25g/1oz grated root ginger
2 garlic cloves, roughly chopped
2 tsp Kashmiri red chilli powder or
  paprika (not smoked)
1 large onion, roughly chopped
25g/1oz fresh turmeric root (or
  2 tsp ground turmeric)

For the raita:

2 tbsp good-quality lime pickle
handful of fresh mint
150g thick, strained yoghurt (if
  you can find yoghurt made from
  goat's or sheep's milk, all the
  better)

This melt-in-the-mouth curry works equally well with goat or lamb. Serve with steamed basmati rice, poppadoms and fresh coriander. Any leftover curry will freeze brilliantly, or why not use it to top a pizza (see page 166).

METHOD

To make the curry paste, place 50ml (2fl oz/scant ¼ cup) of the coconut cream, along with the coriander stalks, ginger, garlic, chilli powder, onion and turmeric into a food processor. Blend until you have a smooth puree.

Preheat a large cast-iron casserole dish. Add the coconut oil and slide into the oven to heat through. Tip in your curry paste, along with the curry leaves (if using), and cook for 4–5 minutes until the mixture is cooked out and very fragrant. Keep stirring the mixture really well to ensure it doesn't catch.

Next, add your goat or lamb to the dish, stirring to coat in the mixture. Return to the oven and cook until well sealed, stirring regularly.

Add the remaining coconut cream. Return to the oven and bring to a simmer. Use a spoon or spatula to ensure you have gently encouraged all the paste that might have stuck to the bottom of the pan to be incorporated into the sauce.

Now add the coconut milk and tamarind paste, return to the oven and bring to a gentle simmer. Cook for between 90 minutes and 2 hours, or until the meat is tender. Check after 1 hour and give everything a good stir.

For the raita, place the pickle, mint leaves and half the reserved coriander leaves into a food processor and blitz until you have a rough paste. Scrape into a bowl and fold in the yoghurt (if you add the yoghurt to the processor it can split).

When the meat is completely tender and the sauce has thickened and reduced, add the garam masala and check the seasoning. Garnish with the remaining coriander leaves.

Merrilees is a chef, event planner, food consultant and mother of two. Although she has catered fine dining events, she has a simple, no-nonsense approach to food, using seasonal and ethically produced ingredients. Her extensive travels have given her food an eclectic edge, blending cooking techniques from far afield with British produce to create unique recipes.

PIZZA

DOUGH

The aim of this book is very much to showcase the versatility of a wood-fired oven. In other words, to explore the vast array of dishes that can be cooked aside from pizza. However, there's no escaping the fact that everybody loves pizza. If you've taken the plunge and invested in a lovely wood oven, you are undoubtedly going to cook pizza many, many times. And there's no better way to cook them than in your own garden, using homemade dough and your wood oven, with friends and a few tipples there for good measure.

The starting point for a good pizza is always the base. Regardless of the quality and deliciousness of the toppings, if the base isn't right then you won't end up with the best pizza you've ever eaten.

Pizza dough is a varied and complex matter. Whole books have been written on pizza dough alone. Phone apps exist that help you calculate exact weights, hydration levels, flour types, yeast percentages, proving times and suchlike. All very scientific, and I am sure if you were running a pizza shop then all those intricate details would be crucial, but most of us just want a go-to pizza dough recipe that is reliable, produces great results and is easy to make.

The easiest way to knock up pizza dough is in a food mixer with a dough hook attachment. Add your dry ingredients first, then the wet, then mix for 5 to 6 minutes until you have a smooth, soft dough. Remove from the machine and set aside in a bowl to prove for the desired time.

The fun way is to tip all your dry ingredients onto a cool surface (professionals use a marble slab) and form a mound. Make a well in the middle and add the wet ingredients. Gradually incorporate the dry ingredients into the liquid until you form a dough, then knead by hand for a good 10 minutes before covering and setting aside to prove.

YEAST

The three main types of yeast you'll find readily available are instant, dehydrated and fresh.

Instant yeast, also known as quick, fast or easy yeast, can be added directly to the flour mixture without the need for rehydrating before use.

Regular dried yeast looks very similar but must be dehydrated before use. Just add the required amount to the water you will be adding to make the dough, stir well and leave for 10 to 15 minutes. You can add half a teaspoon of sugar or honey to the water to really wake up the yeast and whet its appetite for the bigger job it has ahead.

Fresh yeast is harder to find, but I think it adds more flavour, gives a better rise and produces a stretchier dough. However, it is highly perishable and doesn't have the convenience of dried yeast. It must be rehydrated in the same way as dried yeast (above).

The recipes I've listed here use dried yeast. If you'd prefer to use fresh or instant yeast, you'll need to tweak the amount. Use the below chart to work out the equivalent amount for the type of yeast you're using.

Fresh Yeast	Dry Yeast	Instant Yeast
3g	1.5g	1g
6g	3g	2g
10g	4g	3g
12g	6g	4g
17g	7g	5g

MAKING THE DOUGH

Here are three pizza dough recipes that I use on a regular basis. They all work in slightly different ways.

THE BEST OF BOTH WORLDS

This recipe calls for a bit of forward planning as you'll need to start it the day before you cook. The resulting dough is lovely and stretchy, yet fairly easy to handle, and your bases will be crisp, chewy and delicious.

Makes 8 x 30cm/12in pizzas

INGREDIENTS

Day 1
500g/1lb 2oz/4 cups type 00 flour
2 x 7g sachets of dried yeast
600ml/1 pint/2½ cups warm water

Day 2
500g/1lb 2oz/4 cups type 00 flour
20g/¾oz salt
semolina, for dusting

METHOD

On day 1, stir the ingredients together in a large bowl until the mixture reaches a thick batter-like consistency. Cover and leave overnight at room temperature. (If you like to experiment, you can leave the 'batter' in the fridge for 48 hours for an even tastier, stretchier end result.)

On day 2, a few hours before you plan to cook, add the 'batter' to the rest of the ingredients in a large mixing bowl and knead for 10 minutes, by hand or in a machine with a dough hook attachment.

Cover and set aside for an hour or so until doubled in size.

The dough is now ready to make into dough balls. Form them by hand (see page 168), then dip each one into a bowl of semolina to stop them from sticking together. Place onto a baking tray dusted with a little more semolina.

Set aside until doubled in size (around 45 minutes to 1 hour), then you are good to go.

MY FAVOURITE

This recipe uses a far smaller amount of yeast, cold water instead of warm, and relies on a slow, steady prove. The resulting dough is quite wet and sticky but produces simply epic pizzas. This is a recipe to move onto once you've got the hang of shaping pizza balls, stretching out bases and have generally become a master dough-wrangler.

Makes 8 x 30cm/12in pizzas

INGREDIENTS

1kg/2lb 4oz/8 cups type 00 flour

20g/¾oz salt

3g dried yeast

650ml/1 1/3 pints/2¾ cups cold
 water

semolina, for dusting

METHOD

Mix the ingredients together, then knead for 10 minutes, by hand or in a machine with a dough hook attachment.

Cover and set aside for at least 8 hours.

I like to form loose dough balls (see page 168), dip them in semolina and place them into individual bowls dusted with a little more semolina. If you put them in the same tray, they will all melt together.

Allow the dough balls to double in size (this should take 45 minutes to 1 hour), then it's pizza o'clock!

THE QUICK WAY

Really good pizza dough requires time to prove. Proving allows all the glutens to activate and gives that wonderful stretch. It also makes the pizza crusts pop up and gives the base its chewy texture.

This recipe isn't as stretchy or quite as puffy as the other two, however it is ready to use in just 2 hours, so if you are pushed for time, it will do the job for you.

Makes 5 x 30cm/12in pizzas

INGREDIENTS

560g/1lb 4oz/2½ cups type
 00 flour

10g/¼oz salt

7g sachet of dried yeast

300ml/½ pint warm water

50ml/2fl oz/scant ¼ cup olive oil

semolina, for dusting

METHOD

Add the flour and salt to a large bowl.

In a jug, mix together the dried yeast, water and oil. Wait for 5–10 minutes, or until the liquid starts to bubble, then add to the dry ingredients.

Mix together well, then tip out onto a floured board and knead for 15 minutes. Alternatively, use a food processor with a dough-hook attachment on speed 1 for 10 minutes.

Once the dough is smooth, return to the bowl, cover and leave somewhere warm for about an hour until it has doubled in size. The dough is now ready to make into dough balls (see page 168).

Dip each ball into semolina, then place on a tray dusted with a little more semolina. Set aside until doubled in size.

SHAPING THE DOUGH

Using a dough scraper, tip your proved dough onto a work surface dusted with plenty of semolina. Give it a little bash around to knock out any big air pockets.

Cut the dough into equal-sized pieces. For a 30cm/12in pizza, slightly smaller than a tennis ball (around 200–250g/7–9oz) is a good size.

Cup your hand over each piece of dough and roll in a circular motion to form a ball.

PREPARING THE BASE

I like to have a bowl of semolina to hand, as well as a small spice/flour shaker filled with a 50:50 mix of type 00 flour and semolina.

Take a dough ball and dip each side into the semolina. You can either stretch the dough out over the back of your knuckles or place it down on a pizza peel, well adorned with your flour/semolina mix, and push the edges out to form a circle. Try to leave a 1cm/½in band around the edge where the air pockets are still intact. This will form your crust and it will also act as a small barrier to stop the pizza sauce from spilling over the edge.

TOPPINGS

Once your base is ready, you can add your toppings. Generally, the order is: base, tomato sauce, mozzarella, then other toppings. If you are using tomato sauce, be very careful not to get any on the peel or it will stick as you try and slide the pizza into the oven.

MOZZARELLA AND PIZZA SAUCE

A quick note on mozzarella and pizza sauce. I had the pleasure of spending some time with Franco, a 60-year-old pizzaiolo (master pizza maker) in the south of Italy several years ago and we discussed in some depth the pros and cons of different types of mozzarella, and also the best tomato sauce.

There are two types of mozzarella: the fresh, wet, soft type that comes sealed in a little bag filled with water; and the dryer, harder type that is formed into a block and vacuum-packed. Fresh mozzarella is delicious but, because it contains a lot of liquid, it will make your pizza soggy – we don't want that soaking into our pizza bases. So, instead, use the harder type of mozzarella on your pizzas. But, here's the trick that Franco taught me – cut the mozzarella into cubes and put it through a meat grinder. You'll end up with a crumb texture that is super light, melts beautifully and is very easy to spread over your pizza. Keep the fresh stuff for salads.

If you find yourself really getting into pizza making, I recommend buying a cast-iron hand grinder. They can be picked up for £15 to £20 new, or you might be lucky enough to find one in a second-hand store. It's also possible to get an attachment for most food mixers – I have one that sits on the front of my KitchenAid. Failing that, a cheese grater would be the best approach.

Franco's legendary pizza sauce is equally simple. He finds the very best tinned tomatoes available – real Italian, high-end, gourmet ones – and just lightly blitzes them in a food processor. I, too, now follow this method, although everyone has their own personal favourite, so feel free to use your own. I recently discovered a very good brand of tinned pizza sauce by a company called Mutti. Their tinned tomatoes are of excellent quality, too.

COOKING YOUR PIZZA

With the fire burning nice and hot (around 350°C/662°F), slide your pizza into the oven. Once you see the edge closest to the flame start to puff up, bring the pizza out and rotate it by 90 degrees. Continue this process until the pizza is cooked. To check that the base is nice and crispy, gently lift one side of the pizza with the peel – the pizza should lift as a solid disc and not flop over in the middle.

A NOTE ON AMERICAN PIZZAS

While Italians love pizza, it's probably fair to say that the national dish is pasta – but only by a hair's breadth. In the same vein, the hamburger could be considered the national dish of the United States, but I reckon pizza is a very close second. As with many dishes, regional variations spring up over time and the US has developed its own distinct ways of making pizza, and these vary depending on where you find yourself in the country. Here are my top five:

NEW YORK

Known as a 'pie', this style is probably the closest relative to the classic pizza from Southern Italy. It would have been one of the first iterations seen in the US, after being brought over by immigrants from Naples. It is round, with a relatively thin and chewy crust, and fairly traditional in terms of toppings and seasonings.

BROOKLYN

While sitting within the geographical borders of New York, Brooklyn has developed its own sub-genre of the New York pizza. It aims for a thinner, crispier base than its local rival and is more in line with the kind of pizza I like to make at home.

CHICAGO

Despite being somewhat of a motherland for Italian immigrants, the Chicago gang have taken a pizza and literally turned it on its head. They're baked in deep, round dishes and have more of a pastry-style dough. The cheese goes on first, then the toppings and finally the pizza sauce.

DETROIT

Similar in many ways to the Chicago style, Detroit pizzas are baked in deep dishes, but here they use rectangular ones with, again, the cheese going in first, the toppings and finally the sauce. The dough is quite wet and has more of a focaccia texture when cooked.

CALIFORNIA

In many ways, the California pizza sums up the entire Californian food scene. It is much fresher and more adventurous in terms of ingredients, and has a thinner, more traditional-style base. Expect toppings such as rocket and artichokes to be thrown in with non-traditional ones, such as bone marrow or peanut sauce.

These are all good fun and worth a try at home, but for the purposes of this book, we are sticking with the classic Italian style. As Picasso once said, "Learn the rules like a pro, so you can break them like an artist." In other words, get the basics dialled in before you start going too fancy!

PIZZA CLASSICO

Now that we've covered the basics, we can explore different pizza toppings. Here are the classics – what you'd traditionally expect to find on a pizza – and how to create them.

MARGHERITA

Surely the most famous and popular pizza in the world. I have to say, very little beats a really good margherita.

Topping ingredients:
pizza sauce
mozzarella
basil

Cooking notes:
Add the sauce first, then the mozzarella.

Once cooked, scatter with torn basil leaves.

FIORENTINA

Some say this pizza was invented as a breakfast pizza in the city of Florence, and I like that idea. Eggs for breakfast – good! Pizza for breakfast – good! Eggs and pizza for breakfast? Awesome! Regardless, it's certainly in my top five pizzas. Be extra careful with the egg, as it can be a little tricky. The technique is to allow the pizza to cook through enough so the base has set, then draw it out of the oven, make a little well in the centre and break in the egg.

I like to slide it back into the oven but keep the pizza on the peel until the egg starts to set. You can then retract the peel and continue cooking as usual. Please try to keep the yolk runny – it's a delight!

Topping ingredients:
pizza sauce
mozzarella
spinach, wilted and
  squeezed of any excess
  liquid
1 medium egg

Cooking notes:
Add the sauce first, then the mozzarella.

Scatter with the wilted spinach and cook until the base has set.

Carefully break an egg into the centre and return to the oven to cook through.

PEPPERONI

Choose good-quality, fiery-hot, authentic Italian pepperoni for this, and try to find one that contains fennel seeds. If yours doesn't contain fennel seeds, a tablespoonful sprinkled over the pizza will do the trick. This is a firm favourite with my two sons.

Topping ingredients:
pizza sauce
mozzarella
pepperoni

Cooking notes:
Add the sauce first, then the mozzarella.

Scatter sliced pepperoni over the top.

FLAVOUR BOMB

A salty, intensely flavoured favourite, this is one for the umami lovers.

Topping ingredients:
pizza sauce
wood-oven roasted
 artichoke hearts
black olives
capers
anchovies

Cooking notes:
Add plenty of sauce. There's no cheese on this one, but by all means add some if you fancy.

Add a scatter of each of the other ingredients on top.

PROSCIUTTO E FUNGHI

A lovely simple one to finish with: beautiful, thin slices of salty prosciutto that will crisp up as they cook, alongside flavoursome mushrooms. It's very popular in Italy to use tinned mushrooms on pizzas, even in the fancy places. Something about the cooking and canning process seems to intensify the flavours, but I still can't quite bring myself to do it at home. If you experiment and find a good brand that works well, let me know!

Topping ingredients:
pizza sauce
mozzarella
prosciutto slices
thinly sliced mushrooms

Cooking notes:
Add the sauce first, then the mozzarella.

Scrunch up the slices of prosciutto slightly (so that they crispy up nicely) and drape them on top.

Scatter over the mushrooms.

PIZZA BIANCA

I always kick off any pizza-making session with a simple bianca. It's a good way to gauge the heat of the oven and they are great to share as little appetizers before the big-gun pizzas arrive later.

Pizza bianca just means 'white pizza'. There are tons of versions, but the main thing is that none of them are topped with tomato sauce. These are my favourite kind of pizzas, as they really allow the rest of the ingredients to show themselves off. As with any pizza, my style here is to keep things simple: just focus on one or two carefully considered toppings and you'll create something truly wonderful.

GARLIC, HERBS AND SALT

The best garlic bread you will ever eat.

Topping ingredients:
garlic puree
fresh herbs of your
  choosing (rosemary and
  sage work best)
Maldon sea salt
olive oil

Cooking notes:
Smear 1–2 tsp of garlic puree over the base of the pizza and scatter with torn herbs.

Once cooked, add a sprinkle of sea salt and a drizzle of olive oil.

CIPOLLA

Red onions are much sweeter than white, and this is emphasized during the cooking of this very simple yet delicious pizza.

Topping ingredients:
garlic puree
generous handful of
  thinly sliced red onion
Maldon sea salt
olive oil

Cooking notes:
Smear 1–2 tsp of garlic puree over the base of the pizza and pile on the onions.

Once cooked, sprinkle with sea salt and a drizzle of olive oil.

PATATA

This is hands down one my favourite pizzas. After being asked the question recently during an interview, I posted a picture of the pizza on Instagram. I was amazed how many people had never heard of it or tried it!

Ideally, you'll boil a few extra Charlotte or new potatoes next time you're cooking them for another meal and then save them in the fridge ready to make this.

Feel free to add some lardo or little crumbs of sausage meat. Capers also work well.

Topping ingredients:
garlic puree
cooked and thinly
  sliced Charlotte or new
  potatoes
rosemary sprigs
Maldon sea salt
olive oil

Cooking notes:
Smear 1–2 tsp of garlic puree over the base of the pizza and scatter over a few slices of potato.

Once cooked, sprinkle with sea salt and a drizzle of olive oil.

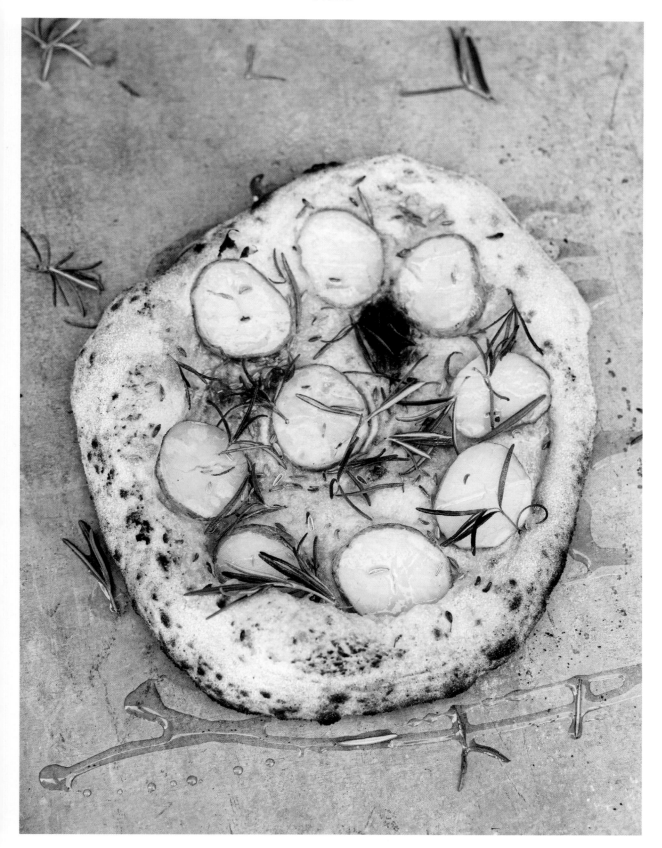

SOUTHERN INDIAN CURRY PIZZAS

RECIPE BY MERILEES PARKER

When I discovered DeliVita's turmeric pizza dough balls, I instantly thought I could do something exciting with them. I had some leftover goat curry kicking around, so the idea of the goat curry pizza was born! Two of my foodie friends tried this invention and were blown away. I've developed the idea a bit further and now sometimes top with roasted cauliflower.

You could always make the curry for one meal and then keep the leftovers in the freezer for the next time you light up your wood-fired oven.

METHOD

Place the curry in a cast-iron pan and place in the oven. Cook until it has thickened and the meat has broken down completely. This will take about 20 minutes but keep an eye on it so that it doesn't catch. Allow to cool completely. This can be done a day ahead.

Make your pizza dough (see page 166) or prepare your shop-bought dough according to the packet instructions.

Take a generous spoonful of the cooled curry (do not warm up beforehand or it will just run off) and spread to about 5cm (2in) from the edge of the pizza base. Cook as described on page 170.

Take the pizza out of the oven, top with roasted cauliflower florets (if you like), drizzle over the raita and sprinkle with coriander leaves. Eat immediately.

TO THICKEN CURRY:
150–200°C
300–482°F

TO COOK PIZZA:
250–330°C
482–626°F

Makes 6

INGREDIENTS

6 shop-bought or homemade
 pizza dough balls (page 168)
½ portion of Southern Indian
 Curry (page 161)

To serve:
1 portion of raita (page 161)
roasted cauliflower florets
 (optional)
coriander leaves

SIDES

ZESTY SPRING GREENS

This is a bright, fresh, zesty accompaniment to fish or meat. Feel free to swap the ingredients for whatever is in season and looking great at the time.

Be careful with the toasted almonds – it turns out they burn like firecrackers if you take your eye off them in the oven! During a recent online wood-fired oven course, I ended up with an inferno in my pan, much to the delight of the participants.

150–200°C
300–400°F

Serves 4

INGREDIENTS

olive oil
100g/3½oz/1 cup flaked
  almonds
handful of baby courgettes (or 2
  medium-sized courgettes)
handful of broad beans, podded
handful of garden peas
approx. 200g/7oz sugar snap peas
  or mangetout
bunch of asparagus
100g/3½oz/¾ cup diced smoked
  pancetta
juice of 1 lemon
freshly ground black pepper

METHOD

In a dry cast-iron skillet, toast the almond flakes until golden brown, then set aside.

Slice the courgettes, sugar snap peas and asparagus into small bite-sized morsels, then mix with the broad beans and peas in a small bowl.

Add the diced pancetta to the skillet with a little oil and slide into the oven to start browning and rendering the fat out. Once golden brown, add the vegetables with approx. 100ml/3½fl oz/scant ½ cup of water and slide into the oven.

Stir regularly until the vegetables are tender but still retain their bite, and the water has virtually gone.

Squeeze in the lemon juice, season with black pepper and transfer to a serving bowl.

Garnish with a generous handful of the toasted almonds.

ROASTED TENDERSTEM BROCCOLI

I'm not a big fan of steamed or boiled sprouting broccoli. The tops overcook and go mushy, while the stems often retain a little too much bite and can be a bit woody. Having said that, I grow lots of broccoli, and that's because, as a family, we love it roasted.

Roasting broccoli brings all the delicious umami, almost Chinese seaweed-like flavours to the forefront, and the smoky char obtained from the wood oven complements it perfectly.

**200–250°C
300–400°F**

Serves 2

INGREDIENTS

large handful of sprouting
 broccoli (purple or green)
rapeseed oil

To serve:
juice of ½ lemon
nigella seeds
Maldon sea salt

METHOD

Preheat a cast-iron pan.

Trim any woody ends from the broccoli stalks.

Toss the broccoli in a little rapeseed oil, just enough to coat, then add to the hot pan.

Cook for 5–6 minutes, turning and moving in the pan regularly. The broccoli should take on a little char and be soft and tender.

Once cooked, transfer to a serving platter, drizzle with lemon juice and a sprinkle of nigella seeds and sea salt.

FRENCH BEANS

**250–330°C
482–626°F**

Serves 2–3

INGREDIENTS

300g/10½ oz/1¼ cups French
 beans, trimmed
rapeseed oil
1 garlic clove, crushed

For the vinaigrette:
3 tbsp rapeseed oil
juice of ½ lemon
2 tbsp finely chopped oregano
Maldon sea salt

To serve:
toasted flaked almonds (see
 page 180)

French beans are quite possibly one of my favourite vegetables. Make sure you buy smaller, younger beans to avoid any unpleasant stringy bits. This is a super-versatile side dish and can accompany pretty much anything.

METHOD

Preheat a cast-iron dish.

Toss the beans in a little rapeseed oil to lightly coat.

Add the beans to the hot dish and cook for 3 minutes. Add the garlic and return to the oven for a further 3–4 minutes, or until just tender (they should still retain their bite).

Meanwhile, make a little vinaigrette by whisking together the rapeseed oil, lemon juice, oregano and sea salt.

Remove the beans from the oven, add the vinaigrette to the dish and toss together until the beans are evenly coated.

Garnish with toasted flaked almonds.

PARMENTIER POTATOES

Parmentier is just a fancy name given to cubed, roasted potatoes. And, because it sounds so fancy, I decided to do some digging. It turns out they're named after the Frenchman Antoine-Augustin Parmentier, who, in the 1770s, championed the potato as a good source of food for humans. Prior to that, potatoes were only used to feed animals, and people used to think they caused leprosy! How times have changed. I can't think of a single vegetable more popular than the humble potato these days. Anyway, on with the recipe...

These make a terrific side for pretty much any main dish. Super-versatile, they should be on regular rotation in your oven. You need to parboil the potatoes for 5 minutes or so before roasting, but it's certainly possible (and even recommended) to do this in advance, allowing them to cool and dry out properly in the fridge.

**150–200°C
300–400°F**

Serves 4

INGREDIENTS

olive oil, for cooking
1kg/2lb 4oz potatoes (Maris Piper,
  King Edward and Marfona all
  work well)
5 garlic cloves
sprig of rosemary

To serve:
Maldon sea salt

METHOD

Peel the potatoes (or leave the skins on and scrub them well) and cut into 2cm (¾in) cubes.

Add to a pot of salted boiling water and cook for 5–7 minutes, or until just starting to soften.

Drain the potatoes and allow them to steam dry for a few minutes.

Add a generous glug of olive oil to a hot cast-iron baking tray. Carefully tip in the potatoes, garlic and rosemary, then mix well.

Slide into the oven and cook for 15–20 minutes, turning and shaking often, until crispy on the outside and soft and fluffy in the middle.

Finish with a sprinkle of sea salt.

YUZU CABBAGE SALAD

Yuzu is an Asian citrus fruit that, looks-wise, is halfway between a lemon and a lime, but tastes incredibly sour. Available from most major supermarkets and Asian grocery stores, it brings a wonderfully fresh and zingy hit when added to dishes.

Yuzu juice is great in salad dressings and stir fries, or anything where you'd usually use fresh lime or lemon juice. Here, we're using it to brighten up an Asian-style slaw.

METHOD

Using a mandoline (or a very sharp knife), thinly slice the vegetables and add to a large serving bowl.

In a separate bowl, mix together the dressing ingredients.

Mix the dressing into the vegetables.

Garnish with a sprinkle of seeds.

Serves 8

INGREDIENTS

½ white cabbage
1 red pepper, deseeded
approx. 200g/7oz/2 scant cups radishes
approx. 150g/5½oz/1 cup mangetout

For the dressing:
150g/5½oz/scant ¾ cup mayonnaise
1 tbsp yuzu juice

To serve:
poppy seeds
toasted sesame seeds

BLACK BEANS

A must-have ingredient in any good taco or burrito, black beans also make a great side dish for grilled meats. The key here is to slow-cook the beans so they break down a little bit and thicken the sauce while cooking. If you like the texture of refried beans, you can smash them up in the pan once cooked until you get a coarse puree consistency.

Feel free to swap the black beans for pinto beans, if you prefer.

METHOD

Add a splash of oil to a cast-iron dish or skillet. Sauté the onion until soft.

Add the cumin, chilli flakes, oregano and salt and mix well.

Add the beans and 500ml (18fl oz/2 cups) stock and give it a good stir.

Allow to cook gently for around an hour, adding more stock if it gets too dry.

**90–150°C
194–300°F**

Serves 8

INGREDIENTS

oil, for cooking
1 onion, diced
1 tbsp ground cumin
1 tsp chipotle chilli flakes
1 tsp ancho chilli flakes
1 tbsp dried oregano
pinch of Maldon sea salt
2 x 400g/14oz cans of black beans,
 drained and rinsed
500–600ml/18fl oz–1 pint/2–2½
 cups vegetable or chicken stock

ROASTED CARROTS
WITH HAZELNUT PICADA

 150–200°C
300–400°F

Serves 4

INGREDIENTS

oil, for cooking
10 smallish heirloom carrots
 of mixed colours, approx.
 1–1.5cm/½–⅝in thick
approx. 70g/2½oz/½ cup
 blanched hazelnuts
4–5 saffron threads (optional)
3 tbsp extra virgin olive oil
1 large garlic clove, crushed
handful of Garlic Croutons
 (page 194)
2 tbsp finely chopped parsley
½ tsp lemon zest

Think of picada as a Spanish pesto: finely chopped or pulverised nuts with olive oil, herbs and garlic, used to jazz up bland dishes, particularly in austere times. The texture of the two are similar, but they taste very different.

As with pesto, picada has been around for centuries and there are countless ways to make it. Often used to thicken stews and soups, some recipes call for bread in the ingredients, but we want to pack as much punch into every mouthful as we can, so we're making use of the Garlic Croutons on page 194.

We're using the picada to add flavour and texture to simple roast carrots – the nuttiness tastes so good with their sweet earthiness. Use heirloom carrots if you can – they taste the same as regular carrots, but they'll look prettier on the plate.

METHOD

Trim the stalks from the carrots and give the skin a scrub with a vegetable brush. Set aside.

Preheat a cast-iron skillet to medium hot in the oven, add the hazelnuts and gently toast until starting to brown. (Be careful not to burn them as they'll taste bitter.)

If you are using saffron, add this to the hazelnuts for the last minute or two of cooking.

Allow to cool, then add the nuts and saffron (if using) to a food processor (or a pestle and mortar). Add the olive oil, garlic, croutons, parsley and lemon zest and lightly blitz – just one or two pulses will do, as you want the texture to remain coarse.

Pour a little oil onto a tray or skillet. Add the carrots and toss to lightly coat in the oil. Slide the tray into the oven.

Roast gently for 15–20 minutes, or until cooked through.

Place the cooked carrots onto a serving dish and spoon over the picada.

GARLIC CROUTONS

**150–200°C
300–400°F**

Serves 2

INGREDIENTS

3 tbsp extra virgin olive oil

3–4 garlic cloves, whole and
  unpeeled

4 slices of sourdough bread (or
  similar robust white loaf), thickly
  sliced (approx. 2–3cm/¾–1¼in
  thick) and torn or cut into
  squarish pieces

Maldon sea salt

freshly ground black pepper

Ideal for topping any salad dish or soup, or just set on the table as a little nibble with drinks.

METHOD

Heat the oil in a cast-iron skillet until shimmering.

Add the cloves of garlic to the pan.

Carefully tip in the bread pieces and quickly mix around so everything is coated in oil.

Slide the skillet back into the oven for a few minutes.

Continue to cook for 7–8 minutes, moving the bread often so all sides get nicely toasted.

Once the bread pieces are crisp and golden, remove and discard the garlic and add the croutons to a mixing bowl.

Season generously with sea salt and a few twists of black pepper.

POTATO SALAD

No outdoor family gathering is complete without a big bowl of homemade potato salad.

Here's my go-to recipe, which adds a few extra flavours. The mustard also gives a lovely colour. New potatoes and Charlotte potatoes both work well.

METHOD

Boil the potatoes until tender. Allow to cool.

Cut the potatoes into bite-sized cubes.

In a large bowl, combine the rest of the ingredients.

Mix in the potatoes.

Serves 4–6

INGREDIENTS

1kg/2lb 4oz firm waxy potatoes
200ml/7fl oz/scant 1 cup
  mayonnaise
1 tbsp natural or Greek yoghurt
1 tbsp American mustard
1 bunch spring onions, finely
  chopped
2 gherkins, finely diced

SAUCES, SEASONING'S & SALSAS

CLASSIC BBQ RUB

This makes a great base rub for pretty much any meat, fish or vegetable heading for your oven. Consider this recipe as a starting point, adding and tweaking as you wish – you could add chilli flakes or citrus zest, perhaps even some fennel seeds.

As a basic rule of thumb, a barbecue rub is:
1 part salt
1 part sugar
1 part smoked paprika
1 part other flavourings (this can consist of whatever you fancy and can be made up of lots of different things).

One thing to be mindful of is that this rub is designed for slow cooking or roasting. If you plan to use it on grilled food, or food cooked hot and fast in the oven, then omit the sugar, keeping the ratios of the other ingredients the same.

Makes approx. 60g/2oz/¼ cup

INGREDIENTS

1 tbsp fine sea salt
1 tbsp white sugar
1 tbsp smoked paprika
½ tsp ground black pepper
½ tsp onion powder or onion salt
½ tsp garlic powder or garlic salt
½ tsp celery salt
½ tsp dried oregano
½ tsp dried parsley

METHOD

Mix all the ingredients together in a small bowl.

Tip into an airtight container. It will keep in a cool, dry place for up to 3 months.

CHIMICHURRI

A pungent garlic, citrus and herb concoction, chimichurri originated in South America. It's amazing with grilled beef, but equally wonderful drizzled over grilled vegetables.

You don't have to follow this recipe exactly. Everyone I know makes their own version – some simpler, some more complex – but at its core, it must include citrus juice, garlic and herbs. After that, you can riff away to your heart's content.

I like to keep chimichurri quite chunky so that it's possible to identify the separate elements and flavours.

METHOD

Mix all the ingredients together in a bowl.

Serves 4–6

INGREDIENTS

4–5 anchovy fillets in olive oil
 (from a jar or can), drained and
 roughly chopped

small handful of capers, drained

1 garlic clove, chopped

2 tbsp white wine vinegar

1 tbsp Dijon mustard

juice of 1 lemon

large bunch of parsley, roughly
 chopped

large bunch of basil, roughly
 chopped

100ml/3fl oz/scant ½ cup olive oil

freshly ground black pepper

PICO DE GALLO

Pico de gallo, meaning 'rooster beak' in Spanish, is a classic Mexican salsa, simply made from five ingredients, plus a little salt. Over the years, it has staked its claim as my go-to topping for any kind of taco, but I also put it into burritos, on top of eggs, use it as a dip – all sorts. Unlike traditional Mexican salsas that tend to be stewed for a little while, pico de gallo always uses raw ingredients, resulting in a much fresher tasting end product.

Some people deseed their tomatoes, so that the salsa is a little less watery. I generally don't, as it's a fiddly job and generally don't feel that the difference it makes warrants the effort.

METHOD

Dice the tomato and onion into roughly ½cm (¼in) cubes and add to a bowl.

Add the jalapeño pepper, coriander and lime juice.

Add a sprinkle of salt and mix well.

Top anything you're eating with a spoonful.

Serves 4

INGREDIENTS

6 large, ripe tomatoes, on
 the vine
½ white onion
1 green jalapeño pepper,
 deseeded and finely chopped
small bunch of coriander,
 chopped
juice of 2 limes
pinch of Maldon sea salt

PINEAPPLE & HABANERO SALSA

250–330°C
482–626°F

Serves 4

INGREDIENTS

1 whole fresh pineapple
juice of 2 limes
1 habanero chilli, finely chopped
small bunch of fresh coriander,
 roughly chopped

Bright, sweet, fresh, citrussy and hot, this is everything you want from a salsa – and dials any taco up to 11.

METHOD

Trim the top and bottom off the pineapple and remove the skin.

Cut the pineapple in half lengthways, then each half into 3, to give you 6 long wedges.

Remove the core from each wedge.

Preheat a cast-iron baking tray in the oven.

Lay the pineapple wedges on the tray and slide into the oven.

Turn every few minutes until the pineapple starts to brown and char a little.

Remove from the oven, allow the pineapple to cool, then dice into 1cm (½in) cubes.

Add to a serving dish, along with the rest of the ingredients, and mix well.

Cover and store in the fridge until needed. The salsa will keep for 2–3 days, but it's best eaten fresh.

SCORCHED SALSA

This is a very versatile dish that can be used as a dip with tortilla chips, a burger topping, incorporated into tacos, or even used to stuff a pork loin. It's quick and easy to prepare and packs a huge punch of flavour. Don't worry if the vegetables char a little bit – that's all part of the fun and will add to the depth of taste.

METHOD

Halve the jalapeño peppers and remove the stalks. (Remove the seeds, too, if you don't want too much heat.)

Add the jalapeños, onion, peppers and cherry tomatoes to a cast-iron dish or tray and drizzle with oil. Slide into the hot oven. Cook until everything starts to char a little bit, tossing regularly.

Remove from the oven and allow to cool for 10 minutes.

Tip everything onto a chopping board, sprinkle with sea salt and lime juice, and finely chop.

Transfer to a bowl and garnish with coriander.

250–330°C
482–626°F

Serves 4

INGREDIENTS

2–3 jalapeño peppers (depending on how hot you like it)
1 red onion, roughly chopped
1 red pepper, deseeded and roughly chopped
1 green pepper, deseeded and roughly chopped
1 small punnet of cherry tomatoes (or 3 round tomatoes)
olive oil
Maldon sea salt
juice of 1 lime

To serve:
small handful of coriander, roughly chopped

BURGER SAUCE

This is the classic diner-style burger sauce. Tangy, sweet and delicious, it's reminiscent of the type you'd find at your local Golden Arches.

This recipe makes about 500ml (18fl oz/2 cups).

METHOD

Combine all the ingredients in a bowl.

Spoon into and onto everything you can think of.

Serves 4

INGREDIENTS

250ml/9fl oz/1 cup mayonnaise
125ml/4fl oz/½ cup ketchup
50ml/2fl oz/scant ¼ cup
  American mustard
2 tbsp very finely chopped
  gherkins
2 tsp very finely chopped shallots
few splashes of Tabasco or Frank's
  Red Hot (or other hot chilli sauce)
few splashes of Worcestershire
  sauce

HOUSE SLAW

A classic house slaw to serve alongside any wood-fired feast. Prepare up to an hour before you plan to eat.

Serves 6

INGREDIENTS

½ red or green pepper, deseeded
 and thinly sliced
½ white cabbage, shredded
1 large carrot, peeled and grated
½ small white onion, thinly sliced

For the dressing:
125ml/4fl oz/½ cup
 mayonnaise
1½ tbsp American mustard
1 tbsp white wine or cider
 vinegar
1 tbsp white sugar

METHOD

Add the pepper, cabbage, carrot and onion to a large bowl.

In a separate bowl, mix up the dressing.

Mix everything together and set aside.

PIMENTÓN OIL

This is a flavour-infused oil that is good to make and keep handy, as it can be used in so many ways. It's great in salad dressings, to use for cooking instead of regular oil, or to drizzle onto meats and vegetables once cooked.

The trick is to heat the oil with the various ingredients and allow them to poach gently for a good half hour. Don't get the oil too hot: simmering or frying will cause unpleasant flavours and bitterness. You can make this in your oven, by all means, but I would suggest a regular hob, as it's a little easier.

Store the oil in a lidded jar or bottle for up to 1 week.

Makes 100ml/3fl oz/scant ½ cup

INGREDIENTS

100ml/3½fl oz/scant ½ cup
 rapeseed oil
2 tsp good-quality Spanish
 smoked paprika
½ tsp dried oregano
½ garlic clove, left whole
2 bay leaves

METHOD

Pour the oil into a pan and add the rest of the ingredients. Mix well.

Heat the oil to around 80°C/176°F.

Maintain the oil temperature for 20–30 minutes.

Strain the oil through a piece of cheesecloth (or a coffee filter) into a clean jar.

SWEET
TREATS

MINI EGG SKILLET BROWNIES
RECIPE BY ELLIE HOWATSON

**90–150°C
194–300°F**

Makes approx. 16

INGREDIENTS

approx. 150g/5½oz/1 cup mini
  chocolate eggs
125g/4½oz/½ cup butter
200g/7oz/1¼ cups dark
  chocolate, roughly chopped
150g/5½oz/¾ cup caster sugar
30g/1oz/¼ cup cocoa, sifted
20g/¾oz/scant ¼ cup flour, sifted
2 large eggs

To serve:
ice cream

You'll also need:
oil or butter for greasing, or
  baking parchment for lining

This recipe is courtesy of my sister-in-law, Ellie, who is the brownie queen of the family.

You need a round skillet, measuring 18–20cm (7–8in) in diameter and without a handle, so you can rotate the brownie in the oven as it cooks.

METHOD

Put the mini chocolate eggs in a ziplock bag and lightly smash them up a bit with a rolling pin – just one or two whacks will do.

Put the butter in a cast-iron dish and slide into the oven to melt.

Put the chopped chocolate, sugar, cocoa and flour in a bowl. Add the melted butter and mix well. Add the eggs one at a time and combine very thoroughly (nobody wants bits of omelette in their brownie).

Add the smashed chocolate eggs and mix.

Prepare your skillet pan by lightly oiling, rubbing with butter or lining with baking parchment. Pour in the mixture, then slide into the oven.

Bake for around 10 minutes until the top has cracked but the brownie underneath still wobbles slightly (don't worry, it will firm up as it cools).

Allow to cool in the skillet for about 15 minutes, then serve with a big dollop of ice cream.

TIP

"THE LAST BATCH I MADE WAS WITH CHOPPED-UP SNICKERS BARS AND PEANUT BUTTER. I PUT THE MIXTURE IN THE TIN AND THEN PUT TWO BIG TABLESPOONS OF PEANUT BUTTER ON TOP AND SWIRLED IT ALL AROUND! THEY WERE AMAZING."
— ELLIE

ROASTED STONE FRUIT
WITH AMARETTI CRUMBLE

Who doesn't love finishing off a meal with a bowlful of crumble? Any stone fruit will work well here (I'd recommend peaches, nectarines or large plums), but whatever fruit you choose, make sure you catch it before it overcooks, or you'll end up with a soggy mess!

METHOD

Slice each fruit from top to bottom and separate into two halves, discarding the stone.

Sprinkle around 1 tsp sugar over the flesh of each half, lay in a dish and slide into the oven to start to soften.

Using a food processor or pestle and mortar, smash together the hazelnuts and amaretti biscuits to a breadcrumb texture (or place in a plastic food bag and smash with a rolling pin).

Remove the fruit from the oven after 5–6 minutes, then place one or two blackberries into each cavity and top with a spoonful of crumble mixture.

Slide back into the oven for about 2–3 minutes, or until the fruit is cooked through and the crumble is golden.

Serve with ice cream, mascarpone or whipped cream.

150–200°C
300–400°F

Serves 4

INGREDIENTS

4 ripe stone fruits
approx. 8 tsp brown sugar
40g/1½oz/¼ cup blanched
 hazelnuts
100g/3½oz amaretti biscuits
8 large (or 16 small) blackberries

To serve:
ice cream, mascarpone or
 whipped cream

GOOEY SKILLET S'MORES

150–200°C
300–400°F

Serves 8

INGREDIENTS

1 x 400g/14oz can of condensed
  milk
150g/5½oz/scant 1 cup dark or
  milk chocolate chips
350g/12oz large American-style
  marshmallows

To serve:
250g/9oz digestive biscuits
400g/14oz strawberries

S'mores are a classic American dessert, with the name coming from a contraction of the words 'some' and 'more'. Traditionally, a marshmallow would be toasted over a campfire, then sandwiched between two Graham crackers. The closest thing we have to Graham crackers in the UK are digestive biscuits, and they work just as well.

This is an eye-spinning sugary hit of a dish, and, with a few simple ingredients, you will be the backyard hero when it gets plonked in the centre of the table. It's especially popular with kids… as you can probably guess.

Keep a close eye on it while it's cooking: it goes from zero to burnt very, very quickly!

METHOD

Pour the can of condensed milk into a cast-iron skillet.

Sprinkle generously with chocolate chips.

Slide the skillet into the oven until the chocolate starts to melt, then mix well.

Stand the marshmallows on their ends on top of the gooey mixture.

Halve your strawberries and assemble on a plate with the digestive biscuits.

Place the skillet into the oven until the marshmallows start to puff up and melt, swirl the mixture around and then slide back into the oven until brown on the top.

Place the skillet on a heat-proof board or trivet and get dipping, using the biscuits and strawberries to scoop up the molten marshmallow mixture. Make your own little sandwich by topping with a second biscuit.

CLASSIC TARTE TATIN

**150–200°C
300–400°F**

Serves 6

INGREDIENTS

flour, for dusting
6 dessert apples, peeled, cored
  and quartered
300g/10½oz all-butter puff pastry
100g/3½oz/½ cup golden caster
  sugar
80g/3oz/⅓ cup cold butter, diced

To serve:
crème fraîche or ice cream

Created by the Tatin sisters at the Hôtel Tatin in the Loire Valley, France, in the 1880s, this surely stands as the Queen of Tarts!

While the classic recipe calls for apples, you can also use a variety of other fruits such as pear, quince, pineapples, peaches and even mango. The tarte Tatin is created by first cooking peeled, cored and quartered apples in a mixture of butter and sugar and then placing puff pastry on top, before hitting the oven for a second time.

Although it means a little more washing-up, I like to use two baking dishes for this. The first to cook the apples and the second to assemble and cook the tart. It helps to stop the whole thing over-caramelizing.

It's important to use regular eating apples rather than cooking apples here. We want the segments to retain their shape and a bit of bite instead of disintegrating into mush. Granny Smith, Golden Delicious, Gala and Braeburn are all good options.

Use a round dish for this, one that you can easily rotate in your oven as it cooks.

METHOD

Place the pastry on a well-floured board. Roll out to a round that is 3mm (⅛in) thick. Chill.

Tip the sugar into a cast-iron baking dish or skillet and slide into the oven to start caramelizing.

Once the sugar has melted and become a dark amber colour, add the butter and mix together to make a caramel.

Add the apples, mix well and slide back into the oven to soften for 5–10 minutes, moving regularly.

Remove from the oven and arrange the apples prettily in a fresh dish, ensuring there are no gaps. Remember, this will be the top of the finished tart.

Pour any remaining caramel over the apples.

Lay the pastry on top, trimming off the excess and tucking the edges around the apples. Prick a few holes in the top to allow the steam to escape.

Slide back into the oven for 25–30 minutes, turning the dish regularly until the pastry is brown and crispy.

Remove from the oven and allow to cool for 1 hour or so.

Run a sharp knife or spatula around the edge to help release the pastry, then invert onto a serving platter.

Serve with crème fraîche or ice cream.

BISCOTTI

Biscotti means 'twice baked' and these Italian biscuits have a reputation for being pretty hard, but that makes them ideal for dunking in coffee. They stand up to submergence in hot liquid far better than some of their British counterparts, such as the Rich Tea, which gives up the ghost after the merest of dips.

However, the last batch I made, I took them out of the oven when the inside was still slightly soft, giving them an almost macaroon-like interior, which was just lovely.

This is a recipe to cook when you've finished with your oven for the day. It is impossible to make biscotti in anything other than a low oven, otherwise the tops will burn and the insides will be raw.

Bake your biscotti on a round tray so that you can rotate it as they cook. If you find the tops are starting to catch, cover it in tin foil until they are cooked through.

 **90–150°C
194–300°F**

Makes approx. 15

INGREDIENTS

75g/2¾oz whole almonds
75g/2¾oz whole hazelnuts
250g/9oz caster sugar
250g/9oz plain flour, sifted
1 tsp baking powder
¼ tsp salt
2 tbsp fennel seeds
grated zest of 1 lemon
2 large eggs

To serve:
icing sugar, for dusting

You'll also need:
baking parchment

METHOD

Preheat a cast-iron skillet in the oven.

Add the nuts to the dry pan and toast for a minute or two until slightly browned. Allow to cool, then roughly chop with a knife or using a food processor.

Place the nuts in a large bowl and stir in the sugar, flour, baking powder, salt, fennel seeds and lemon zest.

Beat the two eggs in a small bowl, then add to the dry ingredients. Mix well until you have a fairly stiff dough. (This will take a few minutes.)

Gently shape your dough into one flattened log or two equal-sized sausages, whichever you prefer. Place onto a cold cast-iron baking tray lined with baking parchment. Carefully trim the parchment around the edge of the biscotti log so that very little is exposed.

Slide the log into the oven, placing it near the doorway, where the temperature is lower.

Cook for 15 minutes, rotating the tray every few minutes, until the top is golden brown.

Remove and carefully check the underside of the log. It should be firm. Set aside to cool (the log will harden slightly as it cools).

Slice the log into 1cm (½in) thick pieces and lay onto the parchment-lined baking tray.

Slide back into the oven for another 5 minutes.

Flip each piece over and return to the oven for a further 5 minutes.

Transfer to a serving platter and dust with icing sugar.

SUPPLIERS

To get the very best out of your wood-fired oven, the basic rule is to start off with great fuel and the highest quality ingredients you can get your hands on.

In my case, I am lucky enough to have a terrific independent butcher nearby, which sells amazing local, free-range meat from animals that have been slowly reared. It's always good to use local butchers – not just because of the quality of the meat, but also because they're in a far better position to supply you with the cut you want. Also, a group of friends in the village set up their own co-operative smallholding, Meat the Flockers, and sell their local, free-range, outdoor-reared, high-quality meat throughout the year.

In terms of vegetables, again, I have a farm shop nearby with very reasonably priced produce, which is grown right next door on their land. Admittedly, the produce is seasonal, but it's a lovely thing to cook in sync with the seasons and make the most of what is fresh and bountiful at that time of year. I also like to use an organic online supplier (details below).

For harder to find ingredients (Mexican or Asian supplies, for example), most decent large supermarkets now have a well-stocked 'world food' section, and there are a handful of specialist online stores I also use. And, of course, there's always the mighty Amazon (amazon.com), but try to buy locally and independently first.

Equipment

Cookware
Alex Pole Ironworks – alexpoleironwork.com
Netherton Foundry – netherton-foundry.co.uk
Nisbets – nisbets.co.uk
Sous Chef – souschef.co.uk

Digital Thermometers
Thermapen – thermapen.co.uk

Fuel & Firelighters
Kindwood – kindwood.co.uk

Knives
Blenheim Forge – blenheimforge.co.uk

Outdoor Cooking Equipment
The Garden Cook – thegardencook.co.uk

Ovens
DeliVita – delivita.com

Tongs
Oxo Good Grips – oxouk.com

Ingredients

Asian
Asianmall – asianmall.co.uk
Starry Mart – starrymart.co.uk

Fruit & Vegetables
Organibox – organibox.org

General
Sous Chef – souschef.co.uk

Italian
Delicatezza – delicatezza.co.uk

Meat
JL Butchers – jl-butchers.co.uk
Meat the Flockers – meattheflockers.square.site
Waghornes Butchers – waghornesbutchers.co.uk

Mexican
Cool Chile Company – coolchile.co.uk

Pepperoni
Properoni – properoni.co.uk

Sauces, Glazes & Rubs
Hot Headz – hot-headz.com
Tubby Tom's – tubbytoms.com

Spanish
Lunya – lunya.co.uk

ABOUT THE AUTHOR

Jon Finch is a live-fire and barbecue cooking expert, food writer and festival maker, based in Gloucestershire, UK. He first started cooking in wood-fired ovens in 2010, at his family home in Puglia, Italy, where he used olive wood straight from the groves and cooked up local delicacies, while learning from the area's expert pizzaioli (pizza makers).

In 2010, Jon founded Bristol's Grillstock Festival, a rip-roaring celebration of barbecue, music and drink, which attracted over 20,000 visitors over the course of its inaugural weekend. In subsequent years, he has produced 12 festivals under the same brand, the largest welcoming 35,000 visitors. The Grillstock brand also grew into a UK chain of five smokehouse restaurants.

Jon has also been involved in a number of other festivals, including the multi-award winning Black Deer Festival in Kent, UK, where he produced and hosted demonstrations on the Live Fire cooking stage.

Jon is now co-owner of Quay Street Diner in Bristol, a vibrant restaurant offering diner classics, from burgers and Po-boys to authentic tacos, and lots of exciting vegetarian and vegan options. He is also a chef for DeliVita and a Weber Grillmaster, giving masterclasses all over the UK. More recently, Jon has launched a series of Fire and Feast experience days, focusing on cooking over firepits.

The author of three cookery books, including bestseller *Grillstock, The BBQ Book* (published by Sphere), Jon has also written articles on barbecue and live-fire cooking for a host of major national publications, including *Olive* magazine, *The Telegraph, The Times, The Independent, Metro, The Guardian, BBC Good Food* and *Shortlist*.

Jon was featured on the only UK episode of *Diners, Drive-Ins and Dives*, hosted by Guy Fieri, and has appeared on *Sunday Brunch, The One Show, BBC Good Food Show* and *This Morning*.

INDEX

ACKNOWLEDGEMENTS

First and foremost, huge thanks go to my own personal cheerleaders – my gorgeous wife, Marie-Louise, and my fabulous sons, Noah and Jakey – for all your support and for allowing me to follow my passions and call it a job. That, and for putting up with me trashing the kitchen on a regular basis.

To my long-standing wingman, Ben, for consistently making me look good over the years. Thanks also for the amazing photos, book design and layout. You are the best.

To Laura Paton, my terrific editor, for your hard work, impeccable organization skills, saint-like patience and willingness to allow me such free reign on the way the book has developed over time.

To Joe and the DeliVita crew for your unswerving passion and enthusiasm for everything I do and your help in making it all happen. You guys are amazing.

To Marcus Bawdon, Merrilees Parker and Dan Toombs – thank you for the delicious guest recipes!

To Jen and George, the best neighbours ever, for putting up with the plumes of woodsmoke drifting into your garden several times a week. And to you, and the rest of the Secret 8, for helping us polish off all the leftovers.

To Dan Cooper for constantly inspiring me as a live-fire chef, and for all your help and support in the background. It's appreciated.

To my publishers at GMC – Jonathan Bailey and Jonathan Phillips – for taking a leap and backing this book.

Finally, the biggest thanks of all to my wonderful parents, Joan and Alec, for giving me a lifelong passion for food and cooking. From a very early age, we always gathered at the table to eat and be merry with friends and family, and it's still my favourite thing to do in the world.

First published 2022 by
Guild of Master Craftsman Publications Ltd
Castle Place, 166 High Street, Lewes,
East Sussex BN7 1XU

Text © Jon Finch, 2022
Copyright in the Work © GMC Publications Ltd, 2022

ISBN 978 1 78494 625 8

Publisher Jonathan Bailey
Production Jim Bulley
Editor Laura Paton
Design and photography Ben Merrington
Additional photography Kris Kirham (p160) and Noah Finch (p169, top)

Colour origination by GMC Reprographics
Printed and bound in China.

FSC
www.fsc.org
MIX
Paper from
responsible sources
FSC® C016973

To place an order, contact: GMC Publications
166 High Street, Lewes, East Sussex, BN7 1XU, United Kingdom
+44 (0)1273 488005